HOSPITALITY MARKETING

DR ANSHUMALI PANDEY

Contents

CHAPTER ONE

INTRODUCTION TO MARKETING

INTRODUCTION:

In the ancient times when people moved ahead from continuous migration to establishing their own settlements they realized that it was difficult to produce everything needed for comfortable life, at the same place. Their interaction amongst themselves to barter basic necessities lead to an understanding that if this interaction would be at a common place with more communities joining in it shall broaden the availability of products and services. This is when the concept of market set in and marketing resulted as an outcome.

The term "marketing" to define commercial activities, buying and selling a product or service was propagated in the late nineteenth century. Historically; Marketing came into existence with the first barter exchange (e.g. the barter trade in ancient Egypt, Songhai and Ghana empires in Africa etc.) when someone realized that exchanges add value for both parties. This was the first real step forward in economic development. Marketing has evolved (like other practices such as architecture, medicine, and engineering) over the centuries to where it is today (Michael Baker).

We are all involved in marketing and: "the enigma of marketing is that it is one of man's oldest activities and yet it is regarded as the most recent of the business disciplines (Baker, 1976).

The concept of marketing can be viewed from social and managerial perspectives. So Marketing is a social and managerial process by which individuals and groups obtain what they need and want through creating and exchanging products and value with others. At its simplest, marketing can be defined as exchange transactions that take place between the buyer and the seller. Marketing is the management function, which organizes and directs all those business activities involved in assessing and converting customer purchasing power into effective demand.

GENERAL DEFINITIONS:

"A market consists of all the potential customers sharing a particular need or want who might be willing and able (i.e., propensity to) to engage in exchange to satisfy that need or want". - Kotler (2004)

A. **Market :** The markets can be of many types e.g. physical consumer markets (the local vegetable market), physical commercial markets (wholesalers, distribution agencies), non-physical markets (e commerce, media markets), financial markets (trade exchanges, stock brokers) and also the illegal trading markets (unauthorized trading).

Market deals with one or more from the following suggestive list:

- Goods
- Services
- Events
- Experiences
- Personalities
- Place
- Organizations
- Properties
- Information
- Ideas and Concepts

B. **Marketing:**

- **Adcock et al:** The right product, in the right place, at the right time, and at the right price"

- **Kotler 1980:** Marketing is the human activity directed at satisfying human needs and wants through an exchange process"

- **Kotler 1991**: 'Marketing is a social and managerial process by which individuals and groups obtain what they want and need through creating, offering and exchanging products of value with others'
- **American Marketing Association**: Marketing is the process of planning and executing the conception, pricing, promotion, and distribution of ideas, goods, and services to create exchanges that satisfy individual and organizational goals.

Marketing is an organizational function and a set of processes for creating, communicating and delivering value to customers and for managing customer relationships in ways that benefit the organization and its stakeholders.

Characteristics of Marketing:

- It yields profits.
- It leads to satisfaction.
- It is ever evolving.
- It is always objective / target based.
- It is an amalgamation of disciplines like economics, sociology, statistical analysis, consumer behavior and management etc.

The concept of marketing revolves around achieving the individual and organizational goals being attained in time to keep ahead of the competitors and to be more effective in creating a brand image with a goal to satisfy the needs, wants and demands of the target markets.

C. **Marketing Management:** Management of marketing activities becomes imperative because the process involves engagement of human resources, capital and additional expenditures incurred to make it result oriented. All these resources need optimum usage as they can be exhausted faster if not monitored properly; thereby leading to losses or lower profit margins.

Philip Kotler: "Marketing Management is the analysis, planning, implementation and control of programmes designed to bring about desired exchanges with target audiences for the purpose of personal and of mutual gain. It relies heavily on the adoption and coordination of product, price, promotion and place for achieving responses."

Marketing management is a business process, to manage marketing activities in profit seeking and nonprofit organizations at different levels of management. Marketing management decisions are based on strong knowledge of marketing functions and clear understanding and application of supervisory and managerial techniques.

- **Peter Drucker:** The first test of any business is not the maximization of profit but the achievement of sufficient profit to cover the risks of economic activity and thus avoid loss.

There is only one valid definition of business purpose: ***to create a customer.***

- It is the customer who determines what business is...
- What the business thinks it produces is not of first importance, especially not to the future of the business and to its success in the market place.
- The customer determines what a business is, what it produces and whether it will prosper.
- Customers are the foundation of a business and their purpose of existence.
- In other words, customers are the mainstay of the business.

D. **HOSPITALITY MARKETING:** Hospitality Marketing differs from generalized marketing as the products and services offered are diverse, intangible, and heterogeneous and have the shortest shelf lives.

Hospitality marketing is collection of efforts focused towards the increase of revenue in the hospitality industry. It deals with various segments of the hospitality industry e.g. hotels, restaurants, resorts, theme parks and other entertainment and accommodations operations promoting their products or services.

The concept of marketing can be viewed from social and managerial perspectives. So Marketing is a social and managerial process by which individuals and groups obtain what they need and want through creating and exchanging products and value with others. At its simplest, marketing can be defined as exchange transactions that take place between the buyer and the seller. Marketing is the management function, which organizes and directs all those business activities involved in assessing and converting customer purchasing power into effective demand.

The American Marketing Association offers the following formal definition: Marketing is an organizational function and a set of processes for creating, communicating and delivering value to customers and for managing customer relationships in ways that benefit the organization and its stake holders. Philip Kotler defines marketing as "a social process by which individuals and groups obtain what they need and want through creating, offering and freely exchanging products and services of value with others". In essence, the marketing concept is customer orientation aimed at generating customer-satisfaction through integrated marketing. Marketing may be narrowly defined as a process by which goods and services are exchanged and the values determined in terms of money prices. That means marketing includes all those activities carried on to transfer the goods from the manufacturers or producers to the consumers.

We shall be learning later in the lesson that marketing is more than a mere physical process of distributing goods and services. It is the process of discovering and translating consumer wants into products and services. It begins with the customer (by finding their needs) and ends with the customer (by satisfying their needs). The components of marketing concept are as under:

a. **Satisfaction of Customers:** In the modern era, the customer is the focus of the organization. The organization should aim at producing those goods and services, which will lead to satisfaction of customers.

b. **Integrated marketing:** The functions of production, finance and marketing should be integrated to satisfy the needs and expectations of customers.

c. **Profitable sales volume:** Marketing is successful only when it is capable of maximizing profitable sales and achieves long-run customer satisfaction.

So, "Marketing is the performance of business activities that directs the flow of goods and services from producer to consumer or user." This definition is undoubtedly an improvement on describing marketing as selling as it shows that marketing does encompass other activities besides selling.

NATURE AND SCOPE OF MARKETING:

Is marketing based on a **scientific method** of inquiry, or is it essentially about an artistic process of creativity? Studies of marketing using the scientific frameworks of the natural sciences have found favor with followers of the **positivist** approach. This holds that, from observations of the real world, it is possible to deduce models that are of general applicability. On this basis, models have been developed to predict consumer behavior, the profitability of retail locations, and price–volume relationships, among many other phenomena.

The great merit of the scientific approach is its claim to great objectivity, in that patterns and trends can be identified with greater confidence than if they were based on casual observation. Many marketers have appreciated the value of this scientific approach. Most major retailers rely heavily on models of retail location before deciding where to locate their next outlet. Armed with trading statistics from their existing network of stores and background information about their locations (e.g. the number of people living within 20 minutes" driving time, passing vehicle traffic per day, proximity to competitors, etc.), a regression model can be developed which shows the significance of each specified factor in explaining sales success. To many people, marketing has no credibility if it does not adopt a rigorous, scientific method of inquiry. This method of inquiry implies that research should be carried out in a systematic manner and results should be replicable: a model of buyer behavior should be able repeatedly to predict consumers" actions correctly, based on a sound collection of data and analysis. In the scientific approach, data are assessed using tests of significance and models are accepted or rejected accordingly.

Marketing cannot possibly copy the natural sciences in its methodologies. Positivist approaches have been accused of seeking meaning from quantitative data in a very subjective manner which is at variance with scientific principles (Brown, 1995). Experimental research in the natural sciences generally involves closed systems in which the researcher can hold all extraneous variables constant, thereby isolating the effects of changes in a variable that is of interest.

For social sciences, experimental frameworks generally consist of complex social systems over which the researcher has no control: a researcher investigating the effects of a price change in a product on demand from customers cannot realistically hold constant all factors other than price. Indeed, it may be difficult to identify just what the „other factors" are that should be controlled for in an experiment, but they may typically include the price of competitors" products, consumer confidence levels, the effects of media reports about that product category, and changes in consumer fashions and Tastes, to name some of the more obvious. Contrast this with a physicist"s laboratory experiment, where heat, light, humidity, pressure, and most other extraneous variables can be controlled, and the limitations of the scientific methodology in the social sciences become apparent.

Marketers are essentially dealing with „open" systems, in contrast to the „closed" systems that are more typical of the natural sciences. Post-positivists place greater emphasis on exploring in depth the meaning of individual case studies than on seeking objectivity and reliability through large sample sizes. Many would argue that such *inductive* approaches are much more customer focused, in that they allow marketers to see the world from consumers" overall perspective, rather than through the mediating device of a series of isolated indicators. Post-positivist approaches to marketing hold that the „real" truth will never emerge in a research framework that is constrained by the need to operationalize variables in a watertight manner. In real-life marketing, the world cannot be divided into clearly defined variables that are capable of objective measurement. Constructs such as consumers" attitudes and motivation may be very difficult to measure and model objectively. Furthermore, it is often the interaction between various phenomena that is of interest to researchers, and it can be very difficult to develop models that correspond to respondents" holistic perceptions of the world.

There is another argument against the scientific approach to marketing, which sees the process as essentially backward-looking. The scientific approach is relatively good at making sense of historic trends, but less good at predicting what will happen following periods of turbulent change. Creativity combined with a scientific approach can be essential for innovation. The scientific approach to marketing planning has a tendency to minimize risks, yet many major business successes have been based on entrepreneurs using their own judgment, in preference to that of their professional advisers. Marketing has to be seen as a combination of art and science. Treating it excessively as an art can lead to decisions that are not sufficiently rigorous. Emphasizing the scientific approach can lead a company to lose sight of the holistic perceptions of its customers. Successful firms seek to use scientific and creative approaches in a complementary manner.

Scope of Marketing:

The scope of marketing can be understood in terms of functions that an entrepreneur has to perform. These include the following:

a. **Functions of exchange:** which include buying and assembling and selling?

b. **Functions of physical supply:** include transportation, storage and warehousing

c. **Functions of facilitation:** Product Planning and Development, Marketing Research, Standardization, Grading, Packaging, Branding, Sales Promotion, Financing.

THE MARKETING CONCEPT:

This concept revolves around the thought that in order to satisfy a client in a market or a guest in hospitality industry everyone who is involved in the process, directly or indirectly and at any stage should move forward with same orientation. E.g. a hotel guest would interact with staff from the front desk, housekeeping, food and beverage services, security, travel etc. in one visit itself and if at one point the interaction is not genuine the efforts of all others are wasted.

Thus, it is clear that if the needs and wants of customers and target markets are understood by putting sincere efforts the efficiency and effectiveness of the process would be far better than those of the competitors.

The hospitality service providers should focus on the demands of target markets; understand the actual demands of guests using the facilities and training their staff to deliver the best in all situations.

Theodore Levitt states three key issues:

1. Organizations must concentrate on the customer and not the product or the company.
2. Organizations should revolve round the customer and not the other way around.
3. The purpose of a business is to create and keep a customer.

The marketing concept holds that the key to achieving organizational goals consists in determining the needs and wants of target markets and delivering the desired satisfactions more effectively and efficiently than competitors. Under marketing concept, the emphasis is on selling satisfaction and not merely on the selling a product. The objective of marketing is not the maximization of profitable sales volume, but profits through the satisfaction of customers.

The consumer is the pivot point and all marketing activities operate around this central point. It is, therefore, essential that the entrepreneurs identify the customers, establish a rapport with them, identify their needs and deliver the goods and services that would meet their requirements. Customers provide payment to an organization in return for the delivery of goods and services and therefore form a focal point for an organization's marketing activity. Customers can be described by many terms, including client, passenger, subscriber, reader, guest, and student. The terminology can imply something about the relationship between a company and its customers, so the term 'patient' implies a caring relationship, 'passenger' implies an ongoing responsibility for the safety of the customer, and 'client' implies that the relationship is governed by a code of ethics (formal or informal).

The customer is generally understood to be the person who makes the decision to purchase a product, and/or who pays for it. In fact, products are often bought by one person for consumption by another, therefore the customer and consumer need not be the same person. For example, colleges must market themselves not only to prospective students, but also to their parents, careers counselors, local employers, and government funding agencies. In these circumstances it can be difficult to identify on whom an organization's marketing effort should be focused.

For many public services, it is society as a whole, and not just the immediate customer, that benefits from an individual's consumption. In the case of health services, society can benefit from having a fit and healthy population in which the risk of contracting a contagious disease is minimized. Different customers within a market have different needs which they seek to satisfy. To be fully marketing oriented, a company would have to adapt its offering to meet the needs of each individual. In fact, very few firms can justify aiming to meet the needs of each specific individual; instead, they target their product at a clearly defined group in society and position their product so that it meets the needs of that group. These subgroups are often referred to as „segments".

NEED:

It is a state of felt deprivation of some basic satisfaction. The state of longing for a basic requirement without which the survival is difficult e.g. food clothes and shelter. With the modern times needs are characterized by the ability to compete thus include additional factors like education, health and entertainment etc. These needs are not pushed instead the consumer is automatically directed to make such purchases.

WANT:

These are wants for specific products that are backed by ability to afford them. The need to satisfy hunger is basic food as per prevalent traditions but an urge to go and have food from a vendor outside becomes a want. Using basic cleanser for soiled utensils like ash, sand and plain water are now replaced by bars and liquids such as Vim and Pril, etc. The water we drink usually is now also available in bottled units which are trendy. The FMCG industry has given a boost to general needs and wants.

DEMAND:

This is the desire for specific satisfiers of our deeper needs and wants. One stage ahead of want is demand when one is capable of higher income generation and is exposed to such culture of spending even when it isn't necessary. The expenditure is incurred not just to satisfy a deeper need but also the ego. E.g. the moving from point A to B in a city is possible by local transport like city bus but in company of colleagues one goes ahead with the use of taxi service.

We can derive that needs, wants and demands are factors that assist a potential customer decide the types of products and services one would use; giving a fair idea to the organization to customize their offerings.

Importance of Marketing:

Since marketing is consumer oriented, it has a positive impact on the business firms. It enables the entrepreneurs to improve the quality of their goods and services.

Marketing helps in improving the standard of living of the people by offering a wide variety of goods and services with freedom of choice, and by treating the customer as the most important person.

Marketing generates employment both in production and in distribution areas. Since a business firm generates revenue and earns profits by carrying out marketing functions,

it will engage in exploiting more and more economic resources of the country to earn more profits.

A large scale business can have its own formal marketing network, media campaigns, and sales force, but a small unit may have to depend totally on personal efforts and resources, making it informal and flexible. Marketing makes or breaks a small enterprise. An enterprise grows, stagnates, or perishes with the success or failure, as the case may be, of marketing. “Nirma” is an appropriate example of the success of small scale enterprise.

PRODUCTS AND SERVICES:

Product: A product is always a tangible item made available to the buyers for use, acquisition or attention. It is anything that can be offered to satisfy a need or a want. This can be sold to a consumer by an individual.

Service: A service is always an intangible offering made available to the buyers to use for a limited period. . This cannot be sold to a consumer by an individual but needs others also to contribute in creating a memorable experience. Thus, a person, place, activity, organization and an idea can be termed as vehicles of services.

Value: This may be defined as the difference between the benefits that the customer gains from owning/ or using a product and the cost of obtaining the product. The values may be related to individual, services, products or image.

Satisfaction: This is dependent on a product's perceived performance in delivering value relative to buyer's expectations. If it does not match customer is dissatisfied, if it matches the customer is satisfied and if it exceeds the customer is delighted.

Quality: It is defined as "freedom from defects" i.e. the ability of a product or a service to satisfy a consumer by virtue of its features and characteristics.

EVOLUTION OF MARKETING:

Marketing has evolved as an important function with time as the service providers have understood that a satisfied consumer would return and also promote the brand thus saving costs and assuring better returns. It has progressed from barter exchanges to e commerce and shopping mall sites where multiple brands are available under one umbrella. This has affected the buying behavior and trends in terms of more money spent in single visit to such places.

Market Orientation / Concepts of Marketing:

Market orientation is the organization-wide generation of market intelligence pertaining to current and future customer needs, dissemination of the intelligence across departments, and organization-wide responsiveness to it (Kohli and Jaworski, 1990).i.e.

a. The process of applying the marketing concept in the market place.
b. Maintaining a customer orientation.
c. All departments work together guided by customer needs/wants/aspirations.

d. Focus on profits/objectives.

According to Narver and Slater (1990), Market orientation comprises three components:

a. Customer orientation
b. Competitor orientation and
c. Interfunctional co-ordination.

The implication of the marketing concept is very important for management. It is not something that the marketing department administers, nor is it the sole domain of the marketing department. Rather, it is adopted by the entire organization. From top management to the lowest levels and across all departments of the organization, it is a philosophy or way of doing business. The customers‘ needs, wants, and satisfaction should always be foremost in every manager and employees' mind. Wal-Mart's motto of "satisfaction guaranteed" is an example of the marketing concept. Whether the Wal- Mart employee is an accountant or a cashier, the customer is always first.

As simple as the philosophy sounds, the concept is not very old in the evolution of marketing thought. However, it is at the end of a succession of business philosophies that cover centuries. To gain a better understanding of the thought leading to the marketing concept, the history and evolution of the marketing concept and philosophy are examined first. Next, the marketing concept and philosophy and some misconceptions about it are discussed.

There are different concepts that guide sellers to conduct their marketing activities. For example sellers can only focus on production and try to reduce their cost of production or focus on improving the quality of the product. Similarly, they can pay more attention to selling and promotion. Therefore, different concepts have evolved to help the organizations to better their marketing activities.

Production Concept (1850-1930):

During the industrial revolution era the focus was on the means of production, and it assumed that the customers will want the product/service being offered. It had no orientation towards incorporating the needs of potential buyers. Majorly the products and services matched the thoughts and perceptions of the manufacturer and the person owning the production unit. It relied on the notion that if a product or service is abundantly available and is of lower cost it is bound to generate sales therefore the focus was on achieving high production efficiency & wide distribution coverage.

Production Concept is a concept where goods are produced without taking into consideration the choices or tastes of the customers. It is one of the earliest marketing concepts where goods were just produced on the belief that they will be sold because consumers need them.

Managers focusing on this concept concentrate on achieving high production efficiency, low costs, and mass distribution. They assume that consumers are primarily interested in product availability and low prices. This orientation makes sense in developing countries, where consumers are more interested in obtaining the product than in its features. Ford, considered as one of the early champions of this concept once remarked that Americans can get any car from Ford until it is black. This is one of the most famous quotes in marketing stressing the importance of Production concept. In a production-orientated business, the needs of customers are secondary compared with the need to increase output. It is natural that the companies cannot deliver quality products and suffer from problems arising out of impersonal behavior with the customers.

For example:

- Coke is widely available throughout the world
- A company manufactures sugar because it knows that in the end consumers will surely buy sugar.

But with the continuous industrialization more and more players entered into the market, the space available to sell the product squeezed because too many people were selling the same product. That is why it became too obvious that the mass production of goods which is the heart and soul of production concept can no longer work because of too many me too products.

Therefore, the focus slightly shifted from Production concept to Customization concept where each and every product is manufactured and delivered according the tastes and choices of the customer. Dell is considered to be the pioneer of this field.

When analyzing this process we can see that since practice makes perfect, workers can carry out the repetitive tasks with great speed and dexterity. Steps can be noted and automated. Employees on the conveyor belt don't need to move around finding tools. However the downside is that boredom sets in as the job is monotonous and recurring.

Members of staff and consumers alike may not feel a sense of pride as identical commodities are being produced.

Product Concept:

This concept shifted focus from bulk production to quality orientation when managers realized that bulk production is not giving enough output for sustainability against increasing competition. Most of the manufacturers were producing similar good in a sector thus the costs went further low and reduced the profit margins. This lead to looking forward to the technical perfection of the product/service seen through the producer's eyes. But here too the assumption that customers will perceive product/service in the same way and thus buy was heavily relied upon. The consumer remained neglected in this phase too.

The product concept proposes that consumers will prefer products that have better quality, performance and features as opposed to a normal product. A company should therefore focus on its product development and invest in continuous product improvements. The concept is truly applicable in some niches such as electronics and mobile handsets.

Two companies which stand apart from the crowd when we talk about the product concept are Apple and Google. Both of these companies have strived hard on their products and deliver us feature rich, innovative and diverse application products and people just love these brands. Managers focusing on this concept concentrate on making superior products and improving them over time. They assume that buyers admire well-made products and can appraise quality and performance. However, these managers are sometimes so proud of their product that they do not realize what the market needs.

One of the advantages of product concepts is that marketers do not need to carry out extensive research into their target audience. Products that a marketer believe will 'sell themselves' do not need a lot of well planned and specifically driven marketing campaigns that can save a company a lot of money.

One problem which has been associated with the product concept is that it might also lead to marketing myopia. For Example, Kodak assumed that consumers wanted photographic film rather than a way to capture and share memories and at first overlooked the challenge of digital cameras. Thus companies need to take innovations and features seriously and provide only those which the customer needs. The customer needs should be given priority.

Sales Concept (1930 to1950):

The sales concept saw efforts moving forward by assuming that consumers have to be coaxed / pushed aggressively to make a decision to buy a certain product or service. The introduction of schemes, benefits, discounts, freebies etc. gave the confidence to sales tem that they can mould a customer and enforce a decision to make a purchase of goods and services offered by their organization. It held the belief that if a customer is free to decide he or she may end up buying only limited numbers. This in reality lead to a situation where the concept of repeat business got hit and companies had to invest more to create attractive products to generate higher sales.

The Selling Concept proposes that customers, be individual or organizations will not buy enough of the organization's products unless they are persuaded to do so through selling effort. So organizations should undertake selling and promotion of their products for marketing success. The consumers typically are inert and they need to be forced for buying by converting their inert need in to a buying motive through persuasion and selling action. The consumers typically show buying inertia or resistance and must be coaxed into buying.

The aim is to sell what they make rather than make what the markets wants. Such marketing carries high risks. It focuses on creating sales transactions rather than on building long term, profitable relationships with customers. This approach is applicable in the cases of unsought goods like life insurance, vacuum cleaner, fire fighting equipments including fire extinguishers. These industries are seen having a strong network of sales force. This concept is applicable for the firms having over capacity in which their goal is to sell what they produce than what the customer really wants. The selling philosophy assumes that a well-trained and motivated sales force can sell any product. However, soon companies began to realize that it is easier to sell a product that the customer wants, than to sell a product the customer does not want. When many companies began to realize this fact, the selling era gave way to the marketing era of the marketing concept and philosophy.

Marketing Concept (1960s onwards):

This was the time when customer got the due attention from the goods manufacturers and service providers. They understood that consumer needs to be given the importance when it comes to designing a new product or service. The focus shifted from owner orientation to identification of customers" needs, redirecting organizational resources and redesigning the objectives. An effort to create an effective match of perceived quality and delivery through market segmentation, targeting, positioning and resource development was introduced.

Let's take an example of 2 eternal rivals – Pepsi and Coke – Both of these companies have similar products. However the value proposition presented by both is different. These companies thrive on the marketing concept. Where Pepsi focuses on youngsters, Coke delivers on a holistic approach. Also the value proposition by Coke has been better over ages as compared to Pepsi which shows that coke especially thrives on the marketing concept, i.e. it delivers a better value proposition as compared to its competitor.

The marketing concept is the most followed ideology by top companies. This is because, with the rise of economy, consumers have become more knowledgeable and choosy as a result of which the organization cannot concentrate on what it sells but rather it has to concentrate on what the customer wants to buy.

The market concept thus relies on three key aspects:

1. **What is the target market** – The first step is to determine exactly what the target market is. This can be done by market research and deciding which target market will give the best returns.

2. **What are the needs wants and demands of the target market** – A further step in marketing research is the consumer preferences study. This study will help the firm determine the needs wants and demands of the

target market thereby helping the firm in deciding their strategies.

3. **How best can we deliver a value proposition** – In this step, the firm decided what strategy it needs to adopt. What kind of value should the firm create and deliver. How should it integrate its different departments? Ultimately, the firm decides how to apply the marketing concept within itself to deliver a better customer experience.

The advent of various categories of hotels and accommodation, food business in different categories are examples of how the organizations made a paradigm shift in strategies to attract more guests and business as a result of it.

The Societal Marketing Concept (1972):

The rising awareness of the customer about his rights and also duties of product offers toward consumers lead to another change. The concept of Social Marketing emerged in 1972, promoting a more socially responsible, moral and ethical model of marketing, countering the consumerism way of thinking that had been promoted by then.

It was introduced in an article by Philip Kotler, "What consumerism means for marketers" in the Harvard Business Review Journal. The social and societal concerns had existed by then, but it was not that they became incorporated explicitly in the marketing literature. Kotler introduced in that period both the concept of Social marketing (extending marketing technologies into non-business areas) and societal marketing, arguing that the marketing concept and its technologies must be tempered and ultimately revised by adopting a more explicit social orientation. His novelty to the marketing concept was the idea of "long-run consumer welfare", emphasizing that the short-term desires might not support the consumer's long term interests or be good for the society as a whole.

This concept holds that the organization's task is to determine the needs, wants, and interests of target markets and to deliver the desired satisfactions more effectively and efficiently than competitors (this is the original Marketing Concept). Additionally, it holds that this all must be done in a way that preserves or enhances the consumer's and the society's well-being. The organization believes in giving back to the society by producing better products targeted towards society welfare. They see it as affording an opportunity for companies to enhance their corporate reputation, raise brand awareness, increase customer loyalty, build sales, and increase press coverage. They believe that customers will increasingly look for demonstrations of good corporate citizenship. This concept is also referred as:

- "The human concept",
- "The intelligent consumption concept",
- "The ecological imperative concept", &
- "Cause- related marketing".

The societal marketing concept calls upon marketers to balance three considerations in setting their marketing policies, viz.

- company profits
- consumer satisfaction
- public interest

Societal Marketing concept focuses on:

- Less Toxic Products
- More Durable Products
- Products with Reusable or Recyclable Material

For example, McDonald may be harming consumer health (due to high fat & salt content in food) & causing environmental problems through the wrappers used in packaging leading to waste & pollution.

Long term interests of the society, its welfare and well-being, sustainability, moral obligations and green thinking were introduced slowly for the companies to be more responsible in their efforts. Corporate Social Responsibility (CSR) activities increased and marginalized sections also got directly benefited in areas like education, living standard up gradation, better housing and health etc.

Consumer Relationship Marketing (CRM) 1990s:

CRM is focused on integration of company's efforts to interact with existing and potential customers using technology. Online communication, direct feedback collection immediately after the use of a product or a service have become almost mandatory. E.g. receiving an automated call from the airline, a tour operator or the railways (139) after the journey is completed for rating the various services offered during the travel.

It results in better synchronization of technology, customer feedback, changes in quality, marketing efforts and end sales. Call centers have been setup with 24X7 services to assist any customers as and when a need arises.

It also tracks client or guest history as in hotels to offer a similar experience on the next visit or the next purchase. This also helps in better forecasting of demand and supply by integration of past trends, figures, sales history etc. with upcoming trends and market conditions.

HOSPITALITY MARKETING:

As the name suggests it is the marketing effort made by hospitality organizations to promote their respective products and services. Hotel Groups, Restaurant Chains, Fast Food Businesses, Banqueting and Event Companies have developed their own strategies and models to enhance sales and also get rated better on customer satisfaction surveys. New offerings like amusement parks, destination weddings, business conferences, ancillary entertainment facilities are becoming a vogue.

Characteristics of Hospitality& Tourism Business:

There are certain characteristic features that make hospitality marketing distinct from general marketing like intangibility, seasonality, inconsistency of demand and delivery by guests and service staff respectively etc. The guests in hospitality industry are more conscious of what is being offered against the price paid for.

1. **Seasonality:** Seasonality affects the hospitality business the most the demand changes with a change in seasons, months of the year, weekdays and weekends, holidays and vacations of family members, and even during the different times an any given day. The maximum

movement happens in Indian hotels between 8 AM to 12 noon. The afternoons and evenings are relatively less crowded as most of the guests have already arrived. The rush in food and beverage service outlets in meal timings is another example of sales and supplies changing within a day"s operation. The demand for hotel accommodations sees an upward trend in vacations when families travel together. Weekend travel with friends has changed the way the clients spend their days in or out of the usual place of residence. The hotels experience peak occupancy in the months of December and January esp. the Christmas and New Year Celebrations. Indian hotels also have unusually high occupancies when the marriage's season sets in. The customers too are more demanding and hotels have to adopt to the demands as this income is add on to business in the year. The challenge for marketing is to increase demand in low season periods and to deflect over-demand from peak periods to other times.

2. **Intangibility:** This features distinguishes hospitality offerings from others substantially as they cannot be experienced– heard, seen, smelt, tasted or touched – prior to being purchased. The guests cannot compare the products and services offered by a hospitality organization on the spot with other brands as in case of buying tangible products like a cell phone or a television from a multi-brand showroom. They have to physically move out and visit the other location or brand to experience the differences. The hospitality businesses have difficulty assessing the quality expected by customers for a similar product or service at two

different times. It is also a challenge to make an offering through the promotional materials that neither raises the expectations to be too high to match nor make it too low to discourage purchases.

3. **Perishability:** A popular saying, "A room lost once is lost forever" appropriately describes the pressure on all employees of a hotel as the numbers of rooms in a hotel, number of covers in a restaurant are fixed. One cannot generate the lost sale on the next day. The hospitality products and services cannot be stored unlike the manufactured goods in a warehouse thus making them hugely perishable. The inventory has to be efficiently managed to counter the fluctuations of demands at any time of the business with keeping guest satisfaction at highest levels. Therefore, the hotels in India usually have a dual tariff system wherein the prices are lower from April to September and revised between October to March. This helps in optimizing the sales when the year-long comparative is done. Hotel room bookings are managed by creating blocks where particular rate, duration and meal package restrictions may be applicable.

4. **Inseparability:** Hospitality products and services cannot be separated in terms of production and consumption. They are produced and delivered at the same time, at the same location but by different individuals. A guest who wishes to experience the hotel accommodation, food services, banquet facility or a discotheque has to come to the venue itself. This leads to the fact that each employee should be very well trained and skilled to handle a hotel guest. Their

interactions are continuous with the guests and may result in a positive or negative influence at any time.

5. **Variability:** It is defined as the change in quality of delivery of a service to a hotel guest by a staff member at various times of operation e.g. the same steward may not be as efficient the beginning and end of a lunch session in a restaurant that witnesses large customer turnover owing to fatigue and continuous demands of clients. Similarly, the product appreciated by one guest may not be appreciated by the other as their preferences may be different despite no change in the quality of product or service offered by the hotel. E.g. same customers order the same meal, which is cooked by the same chef and served by the same staff, in the same restaurant, at the same time of the week. The resulting meal experience can be very different from being perfect one week to being disastrous the next week. Again, two different sets of customers could be served the same meal, at the same time, in the same restaurant and by the same staff, but because of their different knowledge, experience, personal character and feelings, could have very different experiences. A guest's knowledge of hospitality products and services also affects the satisfaction levels e.g. a client knowing the exact temperature of serving a red wine would definitely point it out if there is variation.

6. **Interdependence:** The demand for hospitality products and services is directly dependent on the other variables such as travel arrangements, accommodation, attractions and facilities of a destination. If the customer is satisfied with the hospitality products and services

but not with the other variables there is a lesser possibility of recommending the destinations to other persons though the hospitality operators have delivered the best. The attractions at a destination, infrastructural facilities, word of mouth, overall image of the destination etc. play an important role in influencing the hospitality sector demand. And these two cannot be separated from each other. Thus to accommodate this interdependency all entities have to come together and respond amicably to stabilize the customer satisfaction and demand in return.

7. **Supply exceeds demand:** The ease of entering into hospitality business has directly created competition amongst brands at different levels. Independent hotels, standalone properties at certain places hold major share of business due to varied reasons like historical presence, local influences, authentic food and facilities, unique architecture or simply being the only big player in the market. The government has also encouraged investments in tourism sector esp., in the last two decades where multiple brands have come to India and have changed the quality of services by up skilling of existing staff and by upgrading the existing facilities and standards.

SUMMARY:

This unit has introduced the meaning and nature of marketing that act as building blocks for more detailed discussion in the following units. Having read this unit, you should be aware of the wide definition of marketing and core concept of marketing. Today's successful companies-whether small or large, share a goal of customer satisfaction and are committed to marketing. The marketing comprises many activities- product development, pricing, personal selling, effective channels of distribution, all aimed to achieve profits through customer satisfaction. To be successful in service industry, all the players will have to be strongly market focused. They need to identify market segments since buyers are numerous, widely scattered and different in their needs and preferences. The service product is highly perishable since the supply of services cannot be stored for future use; therefore marketing in service industry is different from marketing of manufactured goods. The service product is developed and other tools of marketing mix are designed to formulate prices, advertising and distribution channels to reach the target market efficiently. Market research helps to design and formulate such a strategy.

You have seen that in the changing market environment with changing customer behavior and seeking business opportunities, companies face marketing challenges on a daily basis. They need to understand the market completely to formulate the best strategy in order to succeed. The core concepts talk about the customers wherein the marketers need to differentiate between the needs, want and demands of a customer. Once this is identified it becomes easier to target the market. It is essential for the organizations to realize the importance of marketing philosophies and which philosophy would suit their business needs. Without studying the environment in which you operate you cannot follow any marketing philosophy.

GLOSSARY:

- **Attitude:** A person's consistently favorable or unfavorable evaluations, feelings, and tendencies toward an object or idea.
- **Customer satisfaction:** The extent to which a product's perceived performance matches a buyer's expectations.
- **Discount:** A straight reduction in price on purchases during a stated period of time.
- **Human Need:** A state of felt deprivation in a person.
- **Human Want:** The form that a human need takes when shaped by culture and individual personality.
- **Inter Functional Coordination** - It is the coordination of all company activities leading to the increase of business performance.
- **Marketing** - A social and managerial process by which individuals and groups obtain what they need and want through creating and exchanging products and value with others.
- **Marketing Concept** – It holds that the key to achieving its organizational goals consists of the company being more effective than competitors.
- **Marketing Concepts:** The marketing management philosophy that holds that achieving organizational goals depends on determining the needs and wants of target markets and delivering desired satisfactions more effectively and efficiently than competitors.
- **Marketing Management:** The analysis, planning, implementation and control of programs designed to create, build and maintain beneficial exchanges with target buyers for the purpose of achieving organizational objectives.

- **Marketing:** A social and managerial process by which people and groups obtain what they need and want through creating and exchanging products and values with others.
- **Price Planning** - Outlines price ranges and levels, pricing techniques purchase terms, price adjustments and the use of price as an active and passive factor.
- **Product Concept** - The product concept proposes that consumers will prefer products that have better quality, performance and features as opposed to a normal product.
- **Product Positioning:** The way the product is defined by consumers" on important attributes- the place the product occupies in consumers" minds relative to competing products.
- **Product:** Anything that can be offered to a market for attention, acquisition, use or consumption that might satisfy want or need. It includes physical objects, services, persons, places, organizations and ideas.
- **Production Concept** - Production Concept is a concept where goods are produced without taking into consideration the choices or tastes of the customers.
- **Quality:** The totality of features and characteristics of a product that bear on its ability to meet customer needs.
- **Selling Concept** - The Selling Concept proposes that customers, be individual or organizations will not buy enough of the organization's products unless they are persuaded to do so through selling effort.
- **Service:** Any activity or benefit that one party can offer to another that is essentially intangible and does not result in ownership of anything.

- **Societal Marketing Concept** - It holds that the marketing activities must be done in a way that preserves or enhances the consumer's and the society's well-being.

CHAPTER TWO

MARKETING ENVIRONMENT, CONSUMER MARKETS & CONSUMER BUYER BEHAVIOUR

INTRODUCTION:

Every day, each of us makes numerous decisions concerning every aspect of our daily lives. However, we generally make these decisions without stopping to think about how we make them and what is involved in the particular decision making process itself. In the most general terms, a decision is the selection of an option from two or more alternatives choices. In other words, for a person to make a decision, a choice of alternatives must be available. When a person has a choice between making, a purchase and not making a purchase, a choice between brand X and Y, or a choice of spending time doing A or , that person is in a position to make a decision. On the other hand , if the consumer has no alternatives from which to choose and is literally forced to make a particular purchase or take a particular action(e.g. use a prescribed medication) then this single , "no-choice" instance does not constitute a decision; such a no-choice decision is commonly referred to as a "Hobson"s choice"

This chapter draws together many of the psychological, social and cultural concepts developed through the book into an overview framework for understanding how consumers make decisions. This chapter also considers consumers" decisions not as the end point but rather as the beginning point of a consumption process.

The personal consumer buys goods and services for his or her own use, for the use of the household or as a gift for friend. Thus the personal consumer may also be referred to as 'end user' or ultimate user because of the fact that he is buying not for selling again. The organizational consumer comprises of profit and non-profit businesses, government agencies and institutions all of which buys to sell their own final product.

The „consumer decision making", which will be studied in detail in the present chapter will be confined only to the first category i.e. decision making by personal consumers. In this context „consumer decision making" may be defined as the process of selecting a product/service to buy from two or more alternative choices by a personal consumer. Hobson's choice or 'no choice decision is beyond the scope of the study of „consumer decision making".

Introduction to Marketing Environment:

Marketing environment includes various factors; both internal and external that assists the organization to build and sustain an effective relationship with its customers in the process of service being offered. In a hotel not just the ambience but also the service attitude of the employees defines basic marketing environment in which operates.

The internal environment is inclusive of employees, promoters, owners, equipment, materials etc. whereas the external environment is made up of variables like society, market conditions, political and social issues, law and government etc. Within these the division of micro and macro environment exists.

On a larger scale the macro marketing environment consists of major components like demographic, economic, physical, technological, political-legal, and social-cultural environment but micro environment consists of variables specific to the business that are external in nature e.g. producing, distributing, and promoting finally delivering it to the consumer for usage.

"A company's marketing environment consists of the actors and forces outside of marketing that affect marketing management ability to build and maintain successful relationships with target customers". – Philip Kotler (12th edition)

Components of Marketing Environment:

A company's marketing environment is made up of the internal and external environment wherein internal environment is controllable but there is much less or at times no control over the external environment.

Internal Environment: Any factor that effects the marketing orientation and results within the organization is a part of internal environment of the business as it directly interacts with the marketing activities.

Five Ms of ahotel"s internal environment are:

1. Men – The Employees / Staff
2. Money – The Capital / Revenue
3. Machinery – The Equipment
4. Materials – The Supplies and Amenities
5. Markets – The Hotel Guests / Sources of Business.

All the above may be altered as per the prevailing external conditions as they are under the control of the team responsible for marketing operations. E.g. if the business season is low due to unfavorable circumstances like hot weather , the team may focus on getting more of residential conference business on rates that suit the hotel and the clients also. This ensures optimum revenue for operations to be run smoothly if not making profits.

External Environment: The external environment comprises of all factors and forces which are external to the business that are not under direct control but have the capability to impact the business revenues. E.g. riots in city push the occupancy levels to lowest. It is studied as micro and macro environment.

MICRO ENVIRONMENT:

All the factors and variables which have a direct correlation with the business like clients, consumers, general publics, business rivals and competitors, resources providers, business generators like travel agents for a hotel make up the micros environment.

For a hotel it can be understood as follows:

- Consumers: Resident and Nonresident Guests, Employees etc.
- Intermediaries & Partners: Travel Agents, Tour Operators, MNCs, Government Organizations, etc.
- Suppliers: Vendors for dry and other raw materials, Service providers like software companies for everyday functions.
- Competitors: Hotels in similar categories, competitive brands, standalone properties, Restaurant Chains etc. which have their shares in the market as a whole.

- **Public: Social communities, Nationalities, Religious Beliefs etc.** impact the type of food, themes, festivities and events organized by the hotel. The satisfied customers are a public who have the ability to impact any marketing activity through favorable word of mouth. The consumer rating firms, freelancing product and service evaluation firms, consumer advocates and watchdog groups are examples of publics that may negatively impact the business if they propagate a negative feedback based picture.

- Shareholders: the investors and promoters also suggest and expect the suggestions to be incorporated in various administrative functions.

MACRO ENVIRONMENT:

This is the collection of variables that have multiplier effect i.e. they the entire industry thereby cause a bearing on its constituents. Macro marketing environment is also known as the broad environment. E.g. Brooke Bond and Lipton came together as Lipton Brooke Bond renowned companies in tea and coffee beverages. It can be broadly divided into the following:

Demographic Environment: Demography refers to the study of population which creates a market. It studies the population on the basis of area, size, location, gender, age, occupations, educational background, density, urban and rural, etc. In the hospitality business the knowledge and awareness of potential customers influences the revenues and popularity of a particular brand or service.

Physical Environment: This relates to the physiology of the place and its conduciveness to operating a business. An easy availability of ample water would be necessary to set up a water park. Similarly, climatic conditions and local environmental would decide the type of food businesses, entertainment facilities suitable to earn better revenue. E.g. A profitable hotel venture would need ease of availability of raw materials, supplies, manpower and connectivity to the nearby transit points.

Economic Environment: Economic environment talks about the money one can spare to do additional purchases other than the regular expenses done. It also studies how the money is spent, where is it spent and how much money is spent in various heads. These factors include the GDP, GNP, interest rates, inflation, income distribution, government funding and subsidies, and other major economic variables etc. The rise and fall in demand or supply may create a slow down or a boom unexpectedly as low demand leads to people expecting further lowering of prices whereas the hike in prices on increase in demand is comparatively lesser. E.g. the hotels have a gestation period of approximately three to five years as a tax holiday during which they strive to build in reputation and brand image by offering best of services on higher costs too.

Social-Cultural Environment: The social-cultural aspect of the macro environment is made up of the lifestyle, values, culture, prejudice and beliefs of the people. This differs in different regions. The potential buyers may be materialistic, domestic, environment concerned, gender dominated, and spiritual in nature thus a change in type of products and services in demand changes. E.g. If a group has majorly women travelers the demand for guestrooms at lobby level is evident. Their need for a safety and security has to be addressed separately.

Technological Environment: With the changing times and increasing awareness of the hospitality services user the organizations have to remodel themselves as per the technological advancements. The bookings have majorly moved to online platforms and websites thus a hotel not listed in these categories would lose the business. It also helps in faster SWOT Analysis thereby helps preparing for challenges and opportunities.

Political-Legal Environment: The political &legal environment includes laws and government's policies prevailing in the country. It also includes other pressure groups and agencies which influence or limit the working of industry and/or the business in the society. The new laws pertaining to food safety, pollution control, energy saving are affecting the spending of hotels. E.g. any food service establishment mandatorily needs at least one FSSAI trained personnel on every twenty servers.

SIGNIFICANCE OF MARKETING ENVIRONMENT:

The growth or decline of a business depends on carefully studied and understood business environment. The positioning of a firm in a competitive scenario calls for channelized analysis of all factors responsible. E.g. a hotel studies the ARR, ADR, Room Revenue, Occupancy statistics etc. for a clarification of its own positioning and image as compared to other competing hotels in the local markets.

a. **Constant Monitoring and Adaptation:** The companies should keep an eye on changing trends and upgrades in technology, services etc. to develop new strategies and policies to counter any effects on business. Adaptation to changing marketing environments is the only key to hold one's market share.
b. **Understanding Changing Needs:** The business needs to introduce new products and services as per consumer demands to assure return. A hotel with higher percentage of guests returning to stay saves much more in marketing as the cost of inviting and convincing a new guest to stay is higher. E.g. the hotels have introduced services like crèche facility for conference

guests, business delegates and families.

c. **Essential for planning:** A hotelier needs to prepare for the future in terms of occupancy, business variations, upcoming competition in the local vicinity, expected changes in government rulings etc. The marketing team has to develop policies in advance to accommodate any changes that may impact the revenue.
d. **Understanding Guests:** The growing exposure of consumers and abundance of information on hospitality products and services has to be clearly seen to assess the changes in their demands. This also takes care of any differences between the perceptions of the market and the marketer.
e. **Early pick up of Trends:** Marketing environment has to be closely monitored and studied to deliver better output and profits. This also assists in developing error free and effective business plans. A challenge is discovering new market segments as the ever changing scenarios create shifting loyalties of even the regular clients. A hotel with a dedicated Business Floor would definitely attract the business travelers compared to a hotel which has similar services but allocates rooms on all the floors to such guests.
f. **Understanding opportunities:** The brands that enter the markets in early stages have the advantages over the followers. They create a more stabilized base with customers as they serve them with a perception of retention.
g. **Competitor Analysis:** Market segments that are specific to a particular brand become more important with time and get known as niche markets. The hotel brands constantly endeavor to hold these customers and it is not uncommon to find guests returning to the same

hotel for years in a row.

BUYER BEHAVIOUR:

The buyers of any product or service adopt a certain methodology to arrive at the final decisions of making a purchase and the study of these aspects is important for all businesses. In this we study the organizations, groups, societies, communities and individual patterns that influence a buying decision. The need may arise out of curiosity for a student but would be more thought of when a businessman makes a purchase.

Buyer behavior looks into the way different people select the products, how do they gather information, how do they include their own perceptions in selections, what impact does the society have it and the effect of experiences gathered from earlier purchases. It is an attempt to deliver matching products and services to a client's perception based on characteristics, individual and group psychology, social demands as per demographics. Every consumer has the distinctive roles of buyer and user, making it difficult for marketing teams to understand them precisely.

This is actually a decision making process that has to be understood at all levels of a purchase from the idea to its execution. E.g. the hotels in a constant effort to keep their products and services as per guest expectations follow the system of guest history generation. The records are available for reference on the guest's next visits to the property thus it is easier for the hotel to offer the specific type of room, the preferred food choices to the guest. This is also termed as relationships marketing by other FMCG firms wherein they create a constant connect with their customers. Retaining customers is essential thus efforts are made to personalize the services, offer customized products, and sending mailers to regular customers for ensuring the relationship is maintained.

Significance of studying Buyer Behavior:

a. Developing need based products and services.
b. Understanding the variables affecting a buyer's choices.
c. To understand the impact of new strategies and policies.
d. To collect customer feedback.
e. To know why a certain product or service is in demand or goes out of demand.
f. To find out how the society influences a buying decision.
g. To develop the appropriate marketing mix with optimum results.
h. It also helps predict the responses to the new offering made by an organization.
a. To understand the sources through which a potential buyer gathers information.
j. To finalize whether a product or service can be sold individually or has to be sold as a package.

Factors affecting buyer behavior:

Buying behavior gets influenced by multiple factors right from the time when a consumer decides to move ahead with an actual purchase. This terminates at the stage where the customers becomes the actual user and assess the expectations and actual satisfaction from such product or service often studied as post purchased evaluation.

<u>These factors can be classified as follows:</u>

a. **Personal:** A variable that is uniquely associated to an individual who makes a purchase e.g. the buyer's age, gender, beliefs, place and community etc.

b. **Exposure**: The extent of a customer's knowledge about the products, the company, brands etc. Customers who reside in the heart of a city with easy accessibility of markets would have wider choices and takes longer to make a purchase, compared to a buyer who has his residence in suburban or rural areas.

c. **Buying Motive**: Why a consumer decides to make a purchase or why does he /she go for a specific brand, color, or time. The client may have a particular motive like a function in the family or have collective motives like joining others at a function, the budget and ego satisfaction at the same time.

d. **Perceptions**: How a person sees a particular process is important to be understood. It is the process of selecting, organizing and interpreting information inputs to produce meaning. i.e. Client chooses what information is important and how is it to be organized, and interpreted. Information inputs are the sensations received through sight, taste, hearing, smell and touch.

e. **Distortions:** The information assimilated by a buyer gets changed over time because of the new developments, its alignment with the beliefs of the individual, new inputs like advertisements and opinions shared by close friends and family members. The advertisements for look-alike brands or in a particular segment such as hotels or restaurants may alter the person's decision to buy. It may selective also if a consumer gets easily influenced by other or is inflexible in nature.

- **Knowledge:** an informed customer is both easy and difficult to convince but an uninformed consumer gets stuck at few points beyond which no suggestions are welcomed.

- **Selective Retention:** Not everything we see, hear or get to know about can be retained by us thus we remember only the products and services that we regularly use or buy as an asset. In an exhibition a buyer gets exposed to thousands of products but only recalls those which he had an idea about and may make an immediate or deferred purchase.

- **Learning Ability**: In modern day the customer has to be trained to buy or select a particular product or service by giving repetitive introductions. The hotels invite delegates from agencies that are good source of business for Familiarization Tours (Fam Tour) every year just to showcase the new ones.

    - **Attitude**: This is the most significant variable as an individual with a positive attitude takes lesser time to decide the purchase and are always positive towards brand and indirectly assist the companies in generating more revenue.

- **Life Styles and Living Standards**: A person's choices depend on the kind of hobbies and interests one has. Someone may prefer a lavish lifestyle and the other may lead a simpler life though both may be having the capacity to spend higher. This is also affected by the nature of professions people adopt for living. E.g. the spending and billing of an FIT guest is much higher than the GIT guests. FIT travels with self-made plans and has own free budget whereas the GIT or the group travelers are dependent on Tour Operator's itinerary and have opted to travel with the group because of limited budget at hand.

- **Opinion Leaders**: Marketing environment is influenced by people who carry a good reputation in the society as most of their followers would use the products and services recommended by them. At the same time individuals who have excelled in their respective fields are taken on board as brand ambassadors to endorse certain products, thus directly affecting the buying decision of the fans. Many Indian states have taken leading film stars to be brand ambassadors to promote travel and tourism activities in the state. E.g. Amitabh Bachchan who represented Gujarat Tourism.

- **Family**: The buying decisions are also altered by the idea, views and feedback given by family members when it comes to purchasing a product which would be of a common use. Marketing professional need to learn how a family unit affects and modifies the preferences esp. the awareness and authority of head of the family. E.g. Children who constantly move with their parents on their business or conference visits are more likely to go for hotel stays when they travel.

- **Memberships and Affiliations**: These are also known as reference groups as individuals who are a part of any such association are more likely to discuss and then make a decision to go ahead with a purchase. They give importance to the views and perceptions shared by the group members thus a possible change in buying decision may not be ignored.

E.g. various hotel groups and travel companies including airlines issue membership cards with multiple benefits for frequent users. This motivates the members to stick to a particular brand for longer duration.

CONSUMER BUYING PROCESS:

Buying is a sequential process i.e. every buyer moves through different stages of decision making process. The standard buying process has a maximum of six stages as explained by many authors in their books and articles. These steps are summarized here for an easier understanding of the concept.

Stage I. Problem Recognition: The first stage relates to the arousal of a need. The buyer becomes aware of what is required and whether the purchase can satisfy it. The reason for this may be the basic needs in normal routine or it may be influenced by an instant exposure to the product or service.

When we are moving in a market with lot of food stalls and the aroma is spread across we tend to decide to purchase a food product. A good advertisement display may motivate us to purchase a pair of jeans though we may have planned for it.

Stage II. Information Search: All potential buyers do a search for information pertaining to the product or service they identify as satisfier of the need by making use of what they remember and know about it before proceeding with looking for support information from external sources.

A successful information search leaves a buyer with possible alternatives known as the evoked set. E.g. If one is feeling exhausted due to hot sun, he or she would want to go out and drink, thus, evoked set is:

- Soft Beverage
- Lime Water
- Fresh Lime Soda
- Flavored Milk.

Stage III. Evaluation of Alternatives: In this stage the buyer weighs or values the possible alternatives with regard to cost, usage, features, brand value etc. The consumer may go back to earlier stages of search and need identification if these criteria are not met.

A group of college students decides to go for fast food during lunch hours; they would first decide a place suiting the budget and their choice of food. If on arrival at the outlet it is closed or packed they again discuss the alternate and move to a different place.

Stage IV. Purchase decision: The potential customer now decides to select one of the alternatives and also decides on the buying alternatives like product, packaging, vendor or place, method of purchase etc.

Stage V. Purchase: At this stage the individual moves out and executes actual buying but the gap between decision making and buying may be of a varied durations depending on availability of time, money, etc.

Stage VI. Post-Purchase Evaluation: After the purchase is done this stage sets in where actual usage happens and this also leads to the buyer understanding whether the decision was correct. The satisfaction or dissatisfaction after the use and /or consumption assures continuity with the particular brand. The services like warranties, guarantee, after sale services also add to satisfaction derived from the use of the product as they ensure rectification of any issue arising out of post purchase.

FOUR TYPES OF CONSUMER BUYING BEHAVIOR:

A consumer's buying behavior depends on the involvement one has in making the decision to purchase. High involvement would mean high risk and vice versa. The involvement also gets affected by urgency, risk taking ability and situation in which purchase is happening.

A. **Routine Response/Programmed Behavior**: Buying low involvement, frequently purchased low cost items; need very little or no search and decision effort. The purchase is done automatically in most cases. E.g. buying a soft drink, snack foods during meal breaks.

B. **Limited Decision Making**: The buying is done when there is need but not a regular one. It states that buyer invests lesser time to collect relevant information about a brand which is relatively not known or has not been used earlier. E.g. Airport Representatives from the hotels offer the property to the arriving guests directly who have limited time at hand.

C. **Extensive Decision Making:** This type of decision making is visible when the products to be bought are of higher value and higher risk. This also involves taking lot of inputs from peers, seniors and experts in the field. E. g buying a house in not an everyday decision thus before it a lot of consultation, evaluation and screening happens. Extensive decision making also involves all six stages of buying. The decision to start using flights instead of other modes is not easy out of apprehensions and phobia of flying for many.

D. **Impulse buying**: Spontaneous buying or buying on the spot without any thought put into the decision. E.g. having a cup of tea on a roadside kiosk while travelling, or buying cotton candies at a busy junction waiting for the light to turn green.

CONSUMER RELATED MODELS OF 'MAN':

Important consumer related models of man are:

- Economic man
- Passive man
- Cognitive man
- Emotional man

A detailed discussion of these models is as follows:

Economic Man:

Prior to Keynes, economists used to assume that there exist perfect competition in the market. The economic man model is essentially based on this thought of there. One of the assumptions of perfect competition is that buyers and sellers have perfect knowledge of the market. In 'economic man' model also it is assumed that consumer is aware of all available product alternatives. It is further assumed that consumer is having capacity to select the best available alternative. Thus this model assumes that a consumer cannot be be-fooled by marketing activities of the producer. He is portrayed as a person who will always make a rational decision because of his knowledge of the market. The consumer in this model is perceived as 'market maven'. However, in reality the consumers rarely have sufficient information about the product alternatives. Leading social scientists have severely criticized the model on the ground that people are limited by the extent of their knowledge and by their existing values and goals. The present day consumer is operating in the world of imperfect competition. He is overpowered with the alternatives available for any purchase. To know about each and every alternative and to choose the best one is not that easy. Under such circumstances the consumer may have to content with a 'satisfactory decision' rather than a rational decision. Thus one may say that 'economic man' model is too idealistic and too simple.

Passive Man:

Passive man model is exactly opposite .to the 'economic man' model. Here the consumer is portrayed as an irrational rather than rational purchaser. The promotional efforts of marketers can induce him to purchase the needed product/service. This model has depicted consumer as a person who can be manipulated by the marketers at will. The passive man does not possess the knowledge of an economic man. He is not very willing either to pressurize himself by searching various alternatives which can satisfy his need. If such is the situation than shrewd marketers comes into picture and by their efforts they can induce this hesitant man to buy their products or services.

The marketers over the years have relied on 'A(DA (Attention, Interest, Desire, Action) model to influence such 'Passive Man'. They are always trying to gain attention, hold interest, arouse desire and elicit action of the prospective consumers. AID A model is not applicable in case of economic man because he himself is very knowledgeable but in case of Passive Man this model assumes special significance.

Like the 'economic man' model, 'Passive man' model has also invited criticism from the experts. The present day customer cannot be easily manipulated by the marketers. The consumers of today are activity seeking information about product alternatives. They cannot be be fooled by aggressive marketers.

Cognitive Man:

Cognitive man model has portrayed consumer as the one who is seeking and evaluating information about selected brands and retail outlets. Cognitive man is different from both 'economic man' and 'passive man'. He is not the man operating in the environment of perfect competition where buyers have full knowledge of the market. He is also not so passive that he will purchase what the marketers are wanting from him to purchase. In cognitive man model the consumer is depicted as thinking problem solver. The cognitive man is not perfectionist. If he is having sufficient information to make a decent decision perhaps he will go ahead with that decision.

Cognitive man model is more realistic than economic man and passive man model. As a matter of fact cognitive man lies somewhere in between of the two extremes i.e. economic man and passive man. Because of being near to reality the cognitive man model has not invited as much criticism as the earlier discussed models. Even the study of consumer behavior as a subject revolves around the concept of cognitive man.

Emotional Man:

Man is social animal. The feelings of joy, sorrow, fear, love always play an important role in his life. Such feelings have an important say in the purchase decision as well. A person who met with an accident on his newly purchased motor bike may not purchase that brand again although it may happen that fault was somewhere else. The horrifying feeling afterwards may prevent him to go far the same brand again. The 'emotional man' model emphasizes that more than spending time in getting information, current mood and feelings of the consumer will play an important role in decision making. The above four models gives us an idea as to why individuals behave as they do. Every individual purchaser may fall in the scope of one model or the other. Marketers' knowledge of their consumers definitely helps them in framing better marketing strategies.

SUMMARY:

Consumer decision making involves selecting a particular alternative out of the entire available alternative concerning the purchase of a product or a service. The consumer decision making process consists of following stages:

1. Need Recognition
2. Information Search
3. Evaluation of Alternatives
4. Purchase
5. Post Purchase Behavior

GLOSSARY:

- **Attitude**: This is the most significant variable as an individual with a positive attitude takes lesser time to decide the purchase and are always positive towards brand and indirectly assist the companies in generating more revenue.
- **Buying Motive**: Why a consumer decides to make a purchase or why does he /she go for a specific brand, color, or time. The client may have a particular motive like a function in the family or have a collective motives like joining others at a function, the budget and ego

satisfaction at the same time.

- **Competitor Analysis:** Market segments that are specific to a particular brand become more important with time and get known as niche markets. The hotel brands constantly endeavor to hold these customers and it is not uncommon to find guests returning to the same hotel for years in a row.
- **Competitors:** Hotels in similar categories, competitive brands, standalone properties, Restaurant Chains etc. which have their shares in the market as a whole.
- **Constant Monitoring and Adaptation:** The companies should keep an eye on changing trends and upgrades in technology, services etc. to develop new strategies and policies to counter any effects on business. Adaptation to changing marketing environments is the only key to hold one's market share.
- **Consumers:** Resident and Nonresident Guests, Employees etc.
- **Demographic Environment:** Demography refers to the study of population which creates a market. It studies the population on the basis of area, size, location, gender, age, occupations, educational background, density, urban and rural, etc. In the hospitality business the knowledge and awareness of potential customers influences the revenues and popularity of a particular brand or service.
- **Distortions:** The information assimilated by a buyer gets changed over time because of the new developments, its alignment with the beliefs of the individual, new inputs like advertisements and opinions shared by close friends and family members. The advertisements for look-alike brands or in a particular segment such as hotels or restaurants may alter the person's decision to buy. It

may selective also if a consumer gets easily influenced by other or is inflexible in nature.

- **Early pick up of Trends:** Marketing environment has to be closely monitored and studied to deliver better output and profits. This also assists in developing error free and effective business plans. A challenge is discovering new market segments as the ever changing scenarios create shifting loyalties of even the regular clients. A hotel with a dedicated Business Floor would definitely attract the business travelers compared to a hotel which has similar services but allocates rooms on all the floors to such guests.
- **Economic Environment:** Economic environment talks about the money one can spare to do additional purchases other than the regular expenses done. It also studies how the money is spent, where is it spent and how much money is spent in various heads. These factors include the GDP, GNP, interest rates, inflation, income distribution, government funding and subsidies, and other major economic variables etc.
- **Essential for planning:** A hotelier needs to prepare for the future in terms of occupancy, business variations, upcoming competition in the local vicinity, expected changes in government rulings etc. The marketing team has to develop policies in advance to accommodate any changes that may impact the revenue.
- **Exposure**: The extent of a customer's knowledge about the products, the company, brands etc. A customer who resides in the heart of a city with easy accessibility of markets would have wider choices and takes longer to make a purchase, compared to a buyer who has his residence in suburban or rural areas.

- **Extensive Decision Making:** This type of decision making is visible when the products to be bought are of higher value and higher risk. This also involves taking lot of inputs from peers, seniors and experts in the field. E. g buying a house in not an everyday decision thus before it a lot of consultation, evaluation and screening happens. Extensive decision making also involves all six stages of buying. The decision to start using flights instead of other modes is not easy out of apprehensions and phobia of flying for many.
- **External Environment:** The external environment comprises of all factors and forces which are external to the business that are not under direct control but have the capability to impact the business revenues. E.g. riots in city push the occupancy levels to lowest. It is studied as micro and macro environment.
- **Family**: The buying decisions are also altered by the idea, views and feedback given by family members when it comes to purchasing a product which would be of a common use. Marketing professional need to learn how a family unit affects and modifies the preferences esp. the awareness and authority of head of the family. E.g. Children who constantly move with their parents on their business or conference visits are more likely to go for hotel stays when they travel.
- **Impulse buying**: Spontaneous buying or buying on the spot without any thought put into the decision. E.g. having a cup of tea on a roadside kiosk while travelling, or buying cotton candies at a busy junction waiting for the light to turn green.
- **Intermediaries & Partners:** Travel Agents, Tour Operators, MNCs, Government Organizations, etc.

- **Knowledge:** an informed customer is both easy and difficult to convince but an uninformed consumer gets stuck at few points beyond which no suggestions are welcomed.
- **Learning Ability**: In modern day the customer has to be trained to buy or select a particular product or service by giving repetitive introductions. The hotels invite delegates from agencies that are good source of business for Familiarization Tours (Fam Tour) every year just to showcase the new ones.
- **Life Styles and Living Standards**: A person's choices depend on the kind of hobbies and interests one has. Someone may prefer a lavish lifestyle and the other may lead a simpler life though both may be having the capacity to spend higher. This is also affected by the nature of professions people adopt for living. E.g. the spending and billing of an FIT guest is much higher than the GIT guests. FIT travels with self-made plans and has own free budget whereas the GIT or the group travelers are dependent on Tour Operator's itinerary and have opted to travel with the group because of limited budget at hand.
- **Limited Decision Making**: The buying is done when there is need but not a regular one. It states that buyer invests lesser time to collect relevant information about a brand which is relatively not known or has not been used earlier. E.g. Airport Representatives from the hotels offer the property to the arriving guests directly who have limited time at hand.
- **Macro Environment**: This is the collection of variables that have multiplier effect i.e. they the entire industry thereby cause a bearing on its constituents. Macro marketing environment is also known as the broad

environment. E.g. Brooke Bond and Lipton came together as Lipton Brooke Bond renowned companies in tea and coffee beverages. It can be broadly divided into the following:

- **Memberships and Affiliations**: These are also known as reference groups as individuals who are a part of any such association are more likely to discuss and then make a decision to go ahead with a purchase. They give importance to the views and perceptions shared by the group members thus a possible change in buying decision may not be ignored.
- **Micro Environment:** All the factors and variables which have a direct correlation with the business like clients, consumers, general public's, business rivals and competitors, resources providers, business generators like travel agents for a hotel make up the micros environment
- **Opinion Leaders**: Marketing environment is influenced by people who carry a good reputation in the society as most of their followers would use the products and services recommended by them. At the same time individuals who have excelled in their respective fields are taken on board as brand ambassadors to endorse certain products, thus directly affecting the buying decision of the fans. Many Indian states have taken leading film stars to be brand ambassadors to promote travel and tourism activities in the state. E.g. Amitabh Bachchan who represented Gujarat Tourism.
- **Perceptions**: How a person sees a particular process is important to be understood. It is the process of selecting, organizing and interpreting information inputs to produce meaning. i.e. Client chooses what information is important and how is it to be organized,

and interpreted. Information inputs are the sensations received through sight, taste, hearing, smell and touch.

- **Personal:** A variable that is uniquely associated to an individual who makes a purchase e.g. the buyer's age, gender, beliefs, place and community etc.
- **Physical Environment:** This relates to the physiology of the place and its conduciveness to operating a business. An easy availability of ample water would be necessary to set up a water park. Similarly, climatic conditions and local environmental would decide the type of food businesses, entertainment facilities suitable to earn better revenue. E.g. A profitable hotel venture would need ease of availability of raw materials, supplies, manpower and connectivity to the nearby transit points.
- **Political-Legal Environment:** The political &legal environment includes laws and government's policies prevailing in the country. It also includes other pressure groups and agencies which influence or limit the working of industry and/or the business in the society. The new laws pertaining to food safety, pollution control, energy saving are affecting the spending of hotels. E.g. any food service establishment mandatorily needs at least one FSSAI trained personnel on every twenty servers.
- **Public: Social communities, Nationalities, Religious Beliefs etc.** impact the type of food, themes, festivities and events organized by the hotel. The satisfied customers are a public who have the ability to impact any marketing activity through favorable word of mouth.
- **Routine Response/Programmed Behavior:** Buying low involvement, frequently purchased low cost items; need very little or no search and decision effort. The

purchase is done automatically in most cases. E.g. buying a soft drink, snack foods during meal breaks.

- **Selective Retention:** Not everything we see, hear or get to know about can be retained by us thus we remember only the products and services that we regularly use or buy as an asset. In an exhibition a buyer gets exposed to thousands of products but only recalls those which he had an idea about and may make an immediate or deferred purchase.
- **Shareholders:** the investors and promoters also suggest and expect the suggestions to be incorporated in various administrative functions.
- **Social-Cultural Environment:** The social-cultural aspect of the macro environment is made up of the lifestyle, values, culture, prejudice and beliefs of the people. This differs in different regions. The potential buyers may be materialistic, domestic, environment concerned, gender dominated, and spiritual in nature thus a change in type of products and services in demand changes
- **Suppliers:** Vendors for dry and other raw materials, Service providers like software companies for everyday functions.
- **Technological Environment:** With the changing times and increasing awareness of the hospitality services user the organizations have to remodel themselves as per the technological advancements.
- **Understanding Changing Needs:** The business needs to introduce new products and services as per consumer demands to assure return. A hotel with higher percentage of guests returning to stay saves much more in marketing as the cost of inviting and convincing a new guest to stay is higher. E.g. the hotels have

introduced services like crèche facility for conference guests, business delegates and families.

- **Understanding Guests:** The growing exposure of consumers and abundance information on hospitality products and services has to be clearly seen to assess the changes in their demands. This also takes care of any differences between the perceptions of the market and the marketer.
- **Understanding opportunities:** The brands that enter the markets in early stages have the advantages over the followers. They create a more stabilized base with customers as they serve them with a perception of retention.

CHAPTER THREE

DISTRIBUTION CHANNELS, PRODUCT PRICING AND SERVICES STRATEGY

INTRODUCTION:

The reason why an entity enters into any business is to trade the goods and services with not only the local customers but also with the potential buyers who are not reachable directly due to constraints like lack of resources, lack of reach, lack of trading ability, and lack of sound knowledge of trading.

Distribution channels are defined as the chain of intermediaries passing through which the product or service finally reaches the end user. All these include the distributors, wholesalers, retailers who are involved in making the product or services available for purchase by a user. The hospitality products are sold directly and also through the tour operators, travel agents, global distribution systems, hotel reservation systems, centralized reservation systems etc. that qualify as being the distribution channels in hospitality.

We have studied in the previous unit how tiresome and rigorous is the process of product development? It needs a lot of resources in terms of time, money and human resource of different departments (Planning, Product development, Human Resource, Finance, Research and Development, etc.) therefore, the wants to gain as much profit from each product as possible, so that the resources that have been applied can be compensated. But here we need to understand that every product also has a life span. As we have different life span for each human similarly different products also have different life spans.

Humans take birth, grow, become mature and then become sick and aged. We need medicines at this time of our life to regain our health and survive further. If we do not get medicines we may die too out of sickness. Similar is the case with products too. Products are also introduced (launched), then they grow, become mature, reach the stagnation stage and slowly and gradually decline. As humans fall sick and revive with medication, products also become sick (bad performance in the market), the company is required to change the marketing strategy (medicine) to rejuvenate them further.

NATURE AND IMPORTANCE OF DISTRIBUTION SYSTEMS:

Distribution channels are diverse in nature as they may be concerned with either the business directly or with the customer on one to one basis. The systems can be distinguished as B2B or B2C and direct or indirect.

B2B Business-to-Business Distribution: This comprises of the system where the interaction is between a producer and industrial users of raw materials needed for the manufacture of finished products. e.g. a hospitality institution would connect with a travel intermediary for room sales and other revenue generating services on behalf of the hotel.

B2C Business-to-Customer Distribution: This is the system that operates on direct interaction between the producer and the end user. e.g. the hotel sells its products and services through its own network, via the website or through the hotel's own reservation system.

Direct Distribution: A distribution system is categorized as direct when it is communication with the customer directly with no scope for middlemen or intermediaries who also earn on the cost of end user. The restaurant sells its products to the customer directly thus the producer and user interact and get involved in business simultaneously. Any product that is tangible may be directly sold to the consumer.

Indirect Distribution: Whenever a product passes through intermediaries or middlemen before being purchased by the customer the system is known to be indirect distribution. The hotel using GDS would depend on it for sale and GDS further is connected to regional, national or local travel agencies, tour operators, taxi and bus service operators, flight intermediaries etc. But in this channel the rates of products and services are higher compared to direct channels used for distribution.

All the above channels have the following involved at one stage or the other in assuring hospitality sales:

- Wholesaler/Distributor: Global Distribution Systems.
- Direct/Internet: Hotel / Hotel Chain Website.
- Direct/Catalog: Brochures and Magazine Advertisements.
- Direct/Sales Team: The Marketing Team, Reservations, Airport Representatives etc.
- Value-Added Reseller (VAR): The Point of Sale team members at a hotel.
- Consultant: The rating and evaluating agency representatives.
- Dealer: Tour Operators
- Retail: Travel Agents
- Sales Agent/Manufacturer's Rep: The on duty staff e.g. the front desk and food servers.

A successful distribution strategy would be focusing on timely delivering the information and services as per the needs of potential customers by understanding there buying preferences, their customization needs, places or media through which they would comfortably make the purchases, whether there is a need to club certain products and services together as a package, making the guests aware of the new additions to the existing range, etc.

A good distribution channel is created if the business is able to identify natural partners i.e. the channels are already in touch with the clients using a similar product or service. A hotel's natural partners are the travel intermediaries as they are already selling multiple services to their customers. They can easily add a hospitality product to the current assortment. It is also essential to identify the size of the market and the reach the company has in its identified market segments.

Creating an effective distribution channel is similar to the process of developing a sales channel where we identify the right associates, the exact number of associates needed to attain a particular revenue target, the mechanism for sharing the revenues, channelizing reporting and communication and also identifying how the information about the products and services is conveyed to the potential consumers.

There may be a need for training and / or familiarizing the selected associates by inviting them to the hotel to have a personalized experience. The Fam-tours conducted by the hotels for its travel agents, tour operators, key persons looking after accommodation and food service arrangements in respective organizations are an effective tool to achieving revenue targets.

MARKETING INTERMEDIARIES:

CARRYING AND FORWARDING AGENTS: These are the usually bigger budget organizations that enter into trading partnership for transfer of goods from the producer to the next level of intermediaries. They do sell the products or services directly to the end user. These intermediaries have warehouses where the transported good are stored for further distribution. The stocking capacity and transportation network of C&F Agencies gives them an edge in negotiating the costs at which they would purchase from the manufacturer or the producer.

WHOLESALERS AND RETAILERS:

These intermediaries are generally the most important link between the manufacturers and customers. They are in business agreements with C&F Agents or the producers and also have an identified customer base with which they interact regularly.

Wholesalers: A wholesaler is the business entity which can hold larger stock to be sold either to the retailer or to the customer directly. The range of products and services offered is limited to a specific sector like FMCG and Electronics etc. In the hospitality industry the GDS acts as the wholesaler for products and services and also distributing them further to the tour operators.

Characteristic features of wholesaler:

1. Bulk purchase but lower quantities of sale to multiple retailers. GDS block a major share of hotel room business at lower rates and then creates sub agents or network associates like the tour operators to sell them next.
2. Direct purchase from C&F Agents or producers. Hospitality organizations tie up with major tour operators and have predefined rates for their products and services irrespective of the rate disclosed to the potential guests.
3. Availability of full range of a product e.g. a wholesaler of musical goods would stock everything from instruments to support equipment like amplifiers, speakers etc.
4. Capital investment is higher. The GDS and bigger travel operators enter into rate agreements based on

guaranteed number of room nights that have to be paid for whether it is able to sell it to the clients or not.

5. Location is generally centralized or specific to a location in the city or the market area. The offices are usually located in business central areas for ease of connectivity.
6. May provide financial support to the small scale producers or manufacturers in case of product range being different from hospitality.
7. The network of further distribution to retailers is supported by agents who work for the wholesaler for a nominal commission. Travel agents are next level of distributors after tour operators.
8. The retailers are generally given a credit cycle of one month or the facility to clear the earlier bill on the next bill generated. The hotels usually pay the commissions in the first week of the month after calculating the monthly sales done by the tour operator.
9. The wholesaler stores the goods in bulk at product specific storage areas. E.g. non perishables in warehouses and perishables as per standard storage requirements.
10. Risk of products remaining as unsold inventory as they are bought in finished condition, change in demand and supply, change in government regulations, loss or damages.

Retailers: The wholesaler supplies the goods and services to the retailer who is responsible to deliver it to the consumers. In case of hotels the retailers are the small or mid-level travel agents in cities or towns that support the sale rooms and other services to the prospective buyers. They have a wider range of products and services for sale available at their disposal.

Characteristics features of retailers:

1. They are the last point of contact between manufacturer and purchasers. The travel agents and hotel staff at point of sale positions may be considered as the retailers.
2. They are selling the products and services for actual use by the buyer. The front desk staff sells the rooms to walk in guests by being clear and convincing.
3. The range of products and services is slightly larger as compared to the wholesaler. The travel agent offers wide variety of services in shorter durations.
4. They do not store for longer period instead make fresh / new products available with the supply trends in the markets.
5. They are in regular touch with the end users thus are clear about their needs and wants thus keeping the appropriate goods for sale.
6. They may purchase unfinished goods and then give them the final shape.
7. They are constantly updating and training the consumers to explore new things.
8. A retailer has the quality to offer personalized service.
9. The display is always trendy and user friendly.
10. The retailer is in a position to influence the buying decision of the consumer due to direct interaction with them.
11. They also apprise the producers, manufacturers, wholesalers etc. regarding the new demands,

customer feedback and suggestions for n=better products and services for increased sales.

WHAT IS A PRODUCT?

A product is a physical or virtual good sold at a particular price. A product is generally tangible and can be permanently owned by the purchaser.

A service is defined as an intangible offering that can be experienced but cannot be permanently owned by the purchaser.

Hospitality Products: According to Philip Kotler "A product is a bundle of physical services and symbolic particulars expected to yield satisfaction or benefits to the buyer"

According to George Fisk, "Product is a cluster of psychological satisfaction"

a. Accommodation: Boarding & Lodging

- Hotels
- Motels
- Lodges
- Cruise Liners
- Floatels
- Resorts
- Inns
- Serviced Apartments
- Residential Apartments
- Camp Sites
- Government Rest Houses & Dak Bungalows

b. Food & Beverage

- Restaurants
- Fast Food Outlets
- Fine Dine / Specialty Restaurants
- Kiosks
- Coffee-shops
- Pubs
- Bars
- Discotheques
- Night Clubs
- Flight Catering

c. Banqueting

- Marriage Halls
- Conference & Convention Spaces
- Meeting & Board Rooms
- Event Management

d. Recreation & Entertainment

- Snooker & Golf Clubs
- Swimming Pool, Health Club & Spa
- Shopping Arcades
- Taxi & Travel Services
- Tour Facilities

Hospitality Services: According to Kotler "A service is any activity or benefit that one party can offer to another that is essentially intangible and does not result in the ownership of anything. Its production may or may not be tied to a physical product".

According to Stanton “Services are those separately identifiable, essentially intangible activities which provide want satisfaction, and not necessarily tied to the sale of the product or another service. To provide a service may or may not require use of tangible goods. However, when such use is required, there is no transfer of title (permanent ownership) of these tangible goods”.

Examples:

- Library
- Shopping
- Booking & Reservations
- Travel Services
- Mail & Messaging
- Guest Feedback Collection & Service Calls

Travel & Tourism Products:

a. Nature Tourism: These include visiting place that have abundant natural beauty and are soothing for a tourist. Lakes, gardens, hill stations, beaches, waterfalls, etc.
b. Historical Tourism: Monuments, archaeological sites, architectural marvels, ancient ruins, fossil parks, etc.
c. Medical Tourism: Holistic treatment, cheaper clinical and medicinal procedures.
d. Health & Wellness: Spa, Gym, swimming pools, cycling tracks
e. Agri - Tourism: visits to villages during sowing and harvesting seasons.
f. Culture Tourism: Places of traditional & cultural importance.

g. Adventure Tourism: Mountaineering, Hiking, Climbing, white water rafting, bungee jumping etc.
h. Religious Tourism
a. Sports Tourism: Asian Games, Olympics, Common wealth Games, World Cups of various sports, etc.
j. Science Tourism: Exploration sites, Excavation Sites, Understanding phenomenon of scientific origin, etc.

Seven phases of the travel experience:

1. Accumulation of mental images about vacation experiences;
2. Modification of those images by further information
3. Decision to take a vacation trip;
4. Travel to the destination;
5. Participation at the destination;
6. Return home; and
7. Modification of images based on the vacation experience.

PRODUCT CLASSIFICATION:

1. **Consumer Products:** Any product that is used by the buyer or personal need satisfaction is a consumer product.

   - **Convenience Products:** The products or services purchased spontaneously and repetitively by the consumers as and when the need arises. These are low priced, placed at most visible locations.

- **Shopping Products:** This type of product is purchased less frequently & price, quality, sustainability & style are closely evaluated by the consumer. . In case of purchase of these products increased time & effort is made by the customers in collection of information & comparison making. E.g. Household items, Appliances, Hotel Services, Vehicles, etc.

- **Specialty Products:** Any product or service that is delivered or is linked to an established brand is a specialty product. The customization can be done depending on the guest. E.g. a hotel always makes special arrangements when the staff are aware of a guest's birthday, anniversary, etc.

- **Unsought Products:** The product which is not purchased with enthusiasm but out of safety and security needs of the family. E.g. Life Insurance.

2. **Industrial Products:** A product bought by the customer which can be used for manufacturing, finishing, servicing like heavy duty vacuum cleaners or floor polishing machines that are used for cleaner and safer floors.

- **Material & Parts:** All the raw materials, natural products & manufactured materials are included in the category of material & parts.
- **Capital Items:** Those industrial products that assist the production & operation are called capital items.

- **Supplies & Services:** Supplies and amenities for smoother experience, and the post-sale services, collecting guest feedback.

3. **Persons, Organizations, Ideas & Places:** Famous personalities, organizations, new ideas, concepts& places.

PRODUCT LIFE CYCLE:

After the launch of the product the management wants the life of the product enough to earn profit to compensate for the efforts and risks. As the external environment changes the marketing strategy of the product is also modified to maximize the profit. Tourism products are called dying products. Life cycle begins as soon as the products development ends. As per Chaudhary (2011), "Product life cycle is the status of a product on time scale from introduction to end in terms of its sales and profits".

The product life cycle (PLC) is useful for describing how products and market work. But using the PLC concept for forecasting the product performance or for marketing strategies presents some practical problems. E.g. managers usually find it difficult to find out the current life cycle stage and ensuring the factors which will affect them in different life stages. Although PLC concept is there in most of the marketing books still there are few managers who claim that they use this concept in practical life. The reasons for this are that although they do not mention the stage of the life cycle of the product but based on the features shown by them, during a particular time managers take decisions and implement them. Secondly drawing the correct PLC curve for a particular product is very difficult. The PLC is not a predictive tool to determine the length of a product's useful life. It is instead, a means of conceptualizing the effect of the market, the environment, and competition and understanding how that product may react to various stimuli. Once the marketer understands the concept that the products have similar life stages it becomes easier for him to lengthen the stages of the life thus making more profit from each stage.

McDonald's has been able to extend by modifying the product concept. The McDonald's of today is a different concept than the McDonald's of the 1960"s. The menu and the store design are different. McDonald's has evolved from stands with no seating into fast –food restaurants with attractive indoor seating areas and playgrounds for children. The company has also changed its location strategy. In addition to its traditional suburban locations, McDonalds developed international, urban, and institutional locations such as hospitals and colleges. The McDonalds restaurant in the Zurich McDonalds Hotels has a bar serving beer, wine, and mixed drinks. One cannot expect this similar menu in India. In India we have Mc Veggie, Chicken Maharaja Mac, and Chocolate and Strawberry Milk shakes in beverages (instead of wine like Switzerland). One may find Big Spice Paneer wrap to satisfy more of Indian palette.

As per Chaudhary (2011), "Destination is defined as a place that has some form of actual or perceived boundary, such as the physical boundary of an island, political boundaries, or even market created boundaries".

Like most products, destinations have a lifecycle. A destination begins as a relatively unknown and visitors initially come in small numbers restricted by lack of access, facilities, and local knowledge, which is labeled as *Exploration.* As more people discover the destination, the word spreads about its attractions and the amenities are increased and improved (*Development).* Tourist arrivals then begin to grow rapidly toward some theoretical carrying capacity (*Stagnation*), which involves social and environmental limits. The rise from *Exploration* to *Stagnation* often happens very rapidly.

When Product Life Cycle (PLC) is applied on a tourism destination it is called Tourism Area Life Cycle (TALC). Several tourism destinations lost their growth due to lack of expert analysis and advice. The tourists stop going to that destination as a result of which the unemployment increases in the region and further creates social problems. Butler (1980) introduced TALC concept by applying PLC model to tourism. He determined six states under his model these are exploration, involvement, development, consolidation, stagnation and the sixth stage is either decline or rejuvenation.

The duration of these stages depend on competition, marketing strategies, external environmental factors, etc.

FEATURES OF PRODUCT LIFE CYCLE:

Where new product development ends a product life cycle begins. A standard life cycle is bell shaped curve as shown in figure 12.2. A typical product life cycle shows following features -

- Most of the product follow “Bell Shape” (or as some authors say “S Shape”) Product Life Cycle. It is also called growth, slum and maturity pattern. As growth picks up then slums or goes down a bit and then again picks up.

- Some products are short lived (Fashions, fads, trendy night clubs) and do not follow the standard bell or S shaped pattern.
- The shape of the PLC curve is independent of the life span of the product which maybe from a couple of days, weeks, to as long as 100 years or maybe more.
- The steep curve represents a short life cycle.
- Some products may stay in matured stage for a very long period of time. E.g. McDonald"s Burgers, Nirula"s thalis, multi-destinations European package tours, etc. These are those products which give good value for money to the tourist.
- Through proper marketing strategy the life of the product can be prolonged.
- A life cycle can be for a generic product, a specific product or a brand.

Product Life Cycle: Every product or service is valid for a fixed duration as per the type or category. The products usually have an expiry date or the best before date mentioned on the packaging. But the services are sold for a much shorter duration and if they are not used in this duration they can are sold to other individuals.

The idea of the Product Life Cycle was first developed in 1965 by Theodore Levitt in an article entitled “Exploit the Product Life Cycle” published in the Harvard Business Review on 1 November 1965.

Every business needs to stabilize in terms of economic and social acceptance. Its sustainability depends on the quality and continuous improvements as per the feedback received from the users. A constant revenue generation helps the organization to plan for expansion, introduction of new business line, a new product range and also assists in growth plan of its employees.

The common Product Life Cycle has four stages:

1. Market introduction stage.
2. Growth stage.
3. Maturity stage.
4. Saturation and decline stage

Stage I: Market Introduction: This stage is the first introduction of the products and services to a market. The launching is done with much fanfare and enthusiasm to let potential customers have the first looks. At this stage the companies are not focused on maximizing revenue or the consecutive sales but are inclined to create awareness. The exercise behind a successful introduction need substantive inputs in terms of both the cost and time with manpower working day in and out as the processes like conceptualization, development, testing and feedback, alterations and changes and finally the marketing campaigning have to be result oriented.

A hotel or a restaurant would always plan a soft launch before it actually gets into full- fledged operations. This makes it easier for the hotelier to understand and troubleshoot the issues arising out of initial service prepositions. The guests may be offered many facilities and freebies like complimentary cakes, floral bouquets, in room facilities, discounts on health club and spa, discounts on laundry and valet services etc. just to encourage them to experience maximum facilities and services.

This stage also includes finding out suitable markets, technologies, features and specialties of the product and service. The hospitality organizations work on themes, menus, room décor, general aesthetics, standard operating procedures, etc. to ensure that everything falls in place before the hotel starts with all services.

There is minimal competition at this stage thus lower targets are given just to make the team comfortable with the goods in the basket. It is the stg where the evaluation happens and thus any item that does not become popular or pick up sale is dropped and the products that outstand are promoted.

Characteristic features of introduction stage:

- **Product development:** research and development of the basic technology and product concept, defining the product features and quality level.
- **Pricing:** pricing strategy is important as the competitors and potential customers are inquisitive about the new products value and worth.
- **Distribution:** the consumer's acceptance of the product leads to decision on distribution to a wider market. .
- **Promotion:** the marketing team focuses on the customers who are interested to buy repetitively and then mould them into patrons or the regular customers.
- Higher input cost but lower sale price.
- **Low sales volumes** to start.

- **Little or no competition** - competitive manufacturers watch for acceptance/segment growth losses.
- Demand has to be created
- **Customers have to be prompted to try the product.**

Stage II: The Growth Stage: Once a set of customers is aware of a product and they are aware of the benefits they tend to accept it. The company can then expect a period of rapid sales growth; entering the "Growth Stage". Here a business tries to strengthen the brand loyalty to increase market share from fair share.

Profits are determined by enhanced sales volumes as the size of market for a particular product or service grow. They are also influenced by cost reductions due to economies of scale, and perhaps more favorable market prices. Competition in the Growth Stage remains low, although new competitors are expected to enter the market. Whenever any competitors enter the market the first challenge an organization faces is change in pricing strategy. The margins go down as the sale prices may have to be brought down without compromising on the quality.

Characteristic features of The Growth Stage:

a. **Product improvement:** Additional features are introduced at this stage and inclusion of after sale services also happens thus product quality automatically gets better. E.g. in a hotel new features like in room on demand music, temperature control before entering the room, self - check in kiosks, touch screens for faster information may be introduced.

b. **Pricing:** Higher demands result in higher prices and vice versa. The hotel tariff changes in peak seasons and is revised in off peak seasons.
c. **Distribution:** It is the right time to add new distribution channels and partners as the demand move upwards. Local and regional travel operators, taxi services are contacted and offered commissions for increasing the reach.
d. **Promotion:** Promotion is aimed at a broader audience thus the business entity may spend a lot of resources on promotion during the Growth Stage.
e. Costs are reduced due to economies of scale.
f. **Higher Sales volume.**
g. Higher Profitability.
h. **Public awareness increases**
i. **Increased Competition** due to a new players entering the established market for that product or service.

Stage III. Maturity Stage: At this stage the sales growth slows and sales volumes eventually peak and become steady. This is the stage during which the market as a whole makes the most profit. A company's key objective at this point is to hold on to its existing market share while maximizing profit. In this stage, prices tend to drop due to increased competition. It is also important to invest more in research and development activities as product quality and efficiency in processes is important to stay ahead of the competition.

Characteristic features of The Maturity Stage:

a. **Product:** Since the presence of competitors makes it tough to sustain the market shares the products need upgrades and unique features to be visible to the customers.
b. **Pricing:** The prices tend to come down in this stage thus an effort should be made to keep them stable and also to stay competitive. We have to study the other business owners for being prepared if a price change is indicated. The seasonal variations in occupancy has to be addressed.
c. **Promotion**: Company's brand, its products and services, its unique selling prepositions should be marketed properly. An effort to be made towards reaching out to more customers should be done e.g. during this stage hotels assure that most of their guests are contacted though various mediums and infirmed about the upcoming programs, events at the hotel. Packages for low seasons have to be created and posted.

d. **Distribution**: The hotel starts offering better incentives and returns to the agencies that bring in bulk business and also starts keeping a track of new agents.
e. Costs are lowered due to new brands or services being provided by competing hotels.
f. Sales volume is at the highest and market saturation is subsequently reached.
g. Increase in competitors entering the market.
h. Brand differentiation and feature diversification is emphasized to maintain or increase market share.

IV. **Saturation and Decline Stage:** This is usually the last stage in a product or service's life after when the prices, profits, sales etc. follow a downward curve and go down to worrying levels if the company has not monitored the transition strategically. The market becomes saturated in terms of total sales and volume of business due to the same quality and features with which it was initially launched. The hotels also experience this change and thus plan for major renovation in themes, aesthetics and facilities offered. Newer brands come in with latest product features thereby reducing the existing market shares and bringing down the productivity. The businesses may adopt the policies like holding, harvesting or divesting. E.g. hospitality firms may add distinctive features, look for new market segments to target or introduce the existing property as new brand in economical segment. It also introduces the training and retraining programs for staff to equip them with new skill sets.

Characteristic features of The Saturation & Decline Stage:

a. **Product**: The Company might start identifying the products and services that are in demand and drop the ones that do not give enough returns. The travel agencies do this by sticking to the properties that give them constant returns and divert their business from the hotels that reduce commissions because of non - popularity of the hotel.

b. **Price**: Lowering of prices may happen as the business may be concerned about inventory and follows the demand patterns.
c. **Promotion**: the high expense low return campaigns are closed and more amounts are diverted to expansion planning, redesigning, finding new avenues etc.
d. **Distribution**: new channels are identified which offer more volume and revenues to balance the losses incurred in case the brand is not modifying the existing products and services according to new markets.
e. **Sales**: Stabilized sales figures and in most cases the sales are reduced.
f. **Profits**: may be marginally reduced as being efficient is more important at this stage.

The product life cycle is a concept that helps the organization identifies the threats and growth opportunities to keep ahead of the growing competition. The products and services offered by hospitality firms shall remain in demand though the quality and variety keeps on changing with new generation demands. E.g. adventure resorts and camping sites are more popular amongst the new tourists.

The hospitality brands like the Marriott, Oberois, Accor, etc. have sustained their market positions despite being in business for so long. Thus the PLC of hospitality industry is slightly different from the FMCG industry as the services offered here have limited shelf life restricted to a day or the operation hours only. All the brands and independent hotels have the freedom to upgrade and introduce new facilities as and when needed to match the customer demands. A good manager should thus be aware of the market positioning of the property and be aware of changing trends to stay in business as the cost of revamping the entire set up is much higher as compared to other daily use goods.

It is therefore clear that product life cycle is a dependent variable and is governed by how a particular market changes its outlook towards the products and services made available by any organization.

MARKETING STRATEGIES DURING DIFFERENT STAGES OF PRODUCT LIFE CYCLE:

Once the product is launched, the management wants to take as much profit from it as possible. The management tries to do this by prolonging the age of the product. Managers know that they cannot expect the product to sell for ever so they want to earn a profit enough to compensate for the efforts done on the product during its development phase. To do this, the strategy is changed several number of times as per the requirements of the market and external environmental condition s as the product moves through the different phases of product life cycle.

DURING EXPLORATION STAGE:

- Practically only a few adventurous tourists, known as early adopters, have visited the destination and there are least tourist facilities, so there are no commercial products available at this stage.

- At this stage, the commercial activities are operated by local communities for the use by local communities only and these facilities are only shared by tourists too.
- Marketing is at a local level as the business is largely handled by local community who do not have resources to advertise products at regional, national or international level.

DURING INVOLVEMENT OR INTRODUCTION STAGE:

Since the product is first offered at commercial level, therefore, it is a very new offering and not much similar matching offers are available in the market. At this stage –

- It is a slow phase. Some products may stay in this phase for years before maturing. E.g. all suite hotels. The companies who do not take risk at this stage and wait for the market to mature may see other becoming the pioneer and taking a larger pie. Proactive players always secure their market share in a better way as compare to late comers.
- The sales growth is slow as the product is not known to the buyers.
- The pioneer gets an excellent market share of the total market available.
- Being a new product, the production cost is usually high.
- Economies of scale cannot be achieved due to limited scale of operation.
- Sales volume and profits are low.
- There is hardly any competition in the market.

- Advertising costs are very high as lot of advertising is required to promote the product.
- Communication is to educate and inform the consumers about the product.
- Initial product may require some changes as and when these are consumed certain components may not fit in as per the nature of the product or may not be liked by the targeted customers.
- If the initial investment is heavy then it acts as a deterrent and the pioneer can enjoy monopoly for longer than expected.
- Setting a pricing strategy at this stage is very difficult. The firm may go for premium prices the recover the cost earlier or may go in for low introductory prices which acts as deterrent for new entrants. But usually prices tend to be on a higher side.
- Usually distribution channels are selected keeping in mind the convenience of the customers.
- Only basic version of the product is launched as the market is not ready for a refined product.
- Heavy sales promotional to try build product trials. This can be done by giving free bees, discounts as a motivation for using product. With type of incentives the product trials are introduced and the product is also well introduced.

DURING DEVELOPMENT OR GROWTHSTAGE:

- Sales start climbing quickly. More competitors enter into the market.

- If there a positive word of mouth then more and more buyers keep on purchasing the product.
- Few competitors start entering the market.
- As competitors also start advertising their products, so the awareness about the destination increases.
- Promotion costs are still high but the strategy shifts from “only spreading awareness” to “fighting with the competition” too.
- Sales as well as profits go high.
- Value addition in the product is done and new feature are added to gain an upper hand in the market.
- Prices have to be made competitive so either will fall only slightly, keeping in mind the image which the company wants to portray of the product. If the competition also enters with a higher or the same price then there may not be any fall in the prices.
- Few channels may be dropped and more may be added, keeping in mind the easy access to the market.
- Processes are standardized to make it convenience to the customers.
- More physical evidences, especially those of real consumers, are added to tangify the product.
- Profit increases as economies companies start achieving economy of scale and sales more efficient systems are developed so miscellaneous costs go down.
- New market segments are entered.
- Advertising starts focusing on product conviction and purchase from product awareness.
- At this stage company is required to choose between a higher market share and higher current profit. Company usually sacrifices profit so that it can reach

to the next level.

- To capture a dominant position in the market company invests a lot on product improvement and product promotion.
- Average cost per customers goes down as expenses although go up but it is distributed in large number of customers.
- The objective is to maximize the market share.
- Product extensions are offered to the market to give more choice to the consumers.
- Sales promotion is reduced and advertising is increased.
- Company goes for intense distribution instead of selective distribution which was followed during the introduction stage.
- Marketers start taking interest in mass market.
- Advertising budget is now directly associated with sales profit. As sales increases the budget for advertising also increases.

DURING CONSOLIDATION OR MATURITY STAGE:

- Sales and profits are maximum at this stage.
- Intense competition can be seen during this stage.
- Marketers try to extend this maturity stage a s much as possible.
- Marketers diversify their product by giving more add on packages and optional tours.
- More distribution channels are added to reach those customers too who are not in reach so far.

- Sales promotion focuses on brand switching.
- Modification and value addition becomes the need of the hour as the competition intensifies with every passing moment.
- Market awareness is done so the focus of communication shifts from fighting with the competition by communicating Unique Selling Prepositions (USPs).
- Prices are reduced further as economy of scale is achieved.
- Prices are reduced to make the product competitive too.
- To increase the reach to the market and to out play the competition more channels are added.
- Promotion costs are still very high as company wants to increase the visibility to beat the competition.
- The focus of promotion shifts from awareness to total experience.

DURING STAGNATION STAGE:

- Market is saturated with players.
- Due to cut throat competition, profit margin per unit is less.
- Due to saturation and low profit margin new competitors don't enter the market at this stage.
- Sale is usually stable and the growth in sales is same as that of the population.
- Only laggards (10 to 12% of all the customers) are left to be trapped.

DURING DECLINE OR PRODUCT DELETIONSTAGE:

- The market loses interest in the product.
- Better options suiting the changing taste enter the market.
- Companies cut down on their profit margin further to attract more customers and increase sale, therefore, gross profit decrease further.
- In spite of price cutting, sales decline further.
- Some marketers start planning to exit from the market.
- Companies having big market share still stay in the marketing hoping that the exit of competitors may increase their sales. These companies sometimes see an increase in the profit.
- Usually Research and development is stopped at this stage to cut the expenditure. Companies accept whatever revenue is generated.
- Like other previous stages promotion costs are high at this stage too. This is so that the market share can be maintained.
- If the decline stage comes earlier then the marketers do not get the return for the efforts and resources he has put in the development and launch of the product that is why companies try to delay this stage as much as they can.
- Expenditure per customer is reduced to reduce the costs.
- Sales promotion is reduced further as most of the customers have already used the product.

DURING REJUVENATION STAGE:

- Some marketers enter into new markets to sell their product. This strategy increases the market share and gross profits.
- Some marketers start finding new uses of the product to increase the sale. E.g. Goa Tourism has started promoting its churches too (Culture Tourism) beside beaches (Nature Based Tourism).
- A product may be at different stages of its life cycle in different markets.
- If the product finds its new use then a new life cycle begins and passes through all the phases of life cycle once again. This is called a second life cycle. It is usually not so good as the first one.

HOSPITALITY SERVICES PRICING:

Hospitality pricing changes as per the targeted market and its specific segments. The grading and classification of hotels and restaurants assures a certain level of quality and the prices to be paid for availing the services. The standard of interiors, final décor, designing, range of services are all depending on the price the guest is willing to pay. The guests at a five star property have expectations of excellent services through highly skilled and trained service professionals thus are ready to pay accordingly. Similarly, when we sit down at the road side tea vendor to have a cup of tea our expectations are limited to a clean utensil to prepare the tea, a clean place to sit and clean glassware to be used for serving the tea.

The difference in pricing of hospitality products can be huge as there are guests who appreciate being treated like the royalty and then there are travelers staying at an inn or a Dharamshalas on a short customary visit to their deities expecting the bare minimum facilities of accommodation and food only.

A downtown or a city hotel would be priced higher than any similar property located in the suburbs of the city. It is the easy connectivity and availability of various services within the vicinity of the city hotel that determines its pricing. A fine dine restaurant would always be costlier as compared to a regular multi-cuisine restaurant as the ambience, services, menu and the staff are all following a common theme which is expensive to maintain.

All the hotel operators have introduced their sub brands catering to specified segment and economy class to assure their presence in the market. E.g. ITC has the range of brands from Sheratons to fortune select hotels catering to their respective segments of luxury and budget clientele.

The hotel firms have rates according to the type of guests also i.e. FIT (Free Individual Traveler) and GIT (Group Individual Traveler). The prices for FIT are in higher side as they are traveling on their own and have the freedom to use all the facilities as per their choices whereas the GIT prices are lower as the guests prefer travelling together to get the advantage of traveling as a group though the services they can avail are limited to the packages they have agreed upon. For any extra services they have to pay separately.

Hospitality pricing can be linked to standard pricing approaches in the following ways:

PRICING FOR NEW PRODUCTS:

- ***Skimming Pricing Strategy:*** The initial price of the products and services is kept very high to ensure that the elite clients are targeted and is presented in such a way that they feel proud to use the brand being introduced. This pricing is suited to the high end traveler and has an intention to capture the market before the competition sets in. The prices are high as the initial expenditure of creating awareness, brand position, brand value and motivating the potential customers is also high. This can also be used in a situation where the markets cannot offer alternative products and services.

- ***Penetration Pricing Strategy:*** The type of pricing is opposite to the skimming pricing as it offers the lowest possible prices in a market during the introduction stages. The price is gradually increased with the change in popularity and demand of the products. This is to ensure that a large share is captured and also to discourage the competition in the beginning. Setting a relatively low price during the initial stages of a product's life. But this strategy can be successful only when the product is favored by a larger segment and gets good response because of the value it offers against the price paid. The demand has to be closely monitored for better return and for sustaining the operational costs.

Pricing for Established Products

- ***Reducing the Price:*** The products and services are already known to the potential customers thus the company launches the same with a lower price tag but at the same time assuring the standard quality. This is practiced to gain a sufficient market share in established markets with a little compromise in the profitability.

E.g. a new hotel in a particular star category launches itself with slightly lower prices to make its presence felt to encourage the guests to visit and experience it. This is a defensive strategy as it reduces the prices in already set price mechanism. In this the company also highlights the uniqueness of the products and services though being offered at lower price. At the same time the property should be ready to compete if the overall market pricing gets lowered.

- ***Increasing the Price:*** The prices may be increased to maintain the profits and revenues in times of inflation in the markets. There is a marginal raise in prices targeted to create and consolidate its existing base of clients. This should be supported by correct use of other marketing policies and strategies simultaneously.

E.g. if a restaurant wishes to increase the prices it should be clear about its base of customers and should be confident that they shall not move to other brands despite the change. The Indian hotel groups like The Taj and The Oberois have a definitive clientele despite the changes in every season as they are confident of getting the best of services.

- ***Maintaining the Price:*** The prices are similar to that of competing brands in the business. This strategy is adopted when we have established and strong competitors in the market who can change their policies just to counter the new entrants. The cost of creating awareness and making the brand visible takes additional cost but it has to be absorbed in the lowered profits.

Other Strategies:

- ***Single Pricing:*** This is the pricing that assures charging the same price to all customers under similar conditions and for the same quantities. This pricing is more suitable to FMCG industry as the hotels do not sell their products and services in bulk. This helps build a goodwill amongst the users and does not induce negative marketing. In the hospitality the hotels of a particular category agree on a common pricing with a negligible variability therefore ensuring a healthy competition.

- ***Flexible Pricing***: The prices may change as per potential customer for the same product or quantity being purchased. E.g. the hotel may offer varying rates for rooms to travel agents depending on the factors like quantum of business, timeliness in payments, cash or deferred payments. A cash paying consumer is always preferred and is offered higher discounts. This also maximizes short-term profits and build traffic by allowing upward and downward adjustments in price depending on competitive conditions and how much the customer is willing to pay for the product. This is suitable only when a firm closely studies the value perceptions for a customer, focuses on profits margins and also keeps an eye on the graphs and trends of how the pricing variations have occurred in the past.

- ***Price Leadership***: This is a strategy adopted by the business entity leading in its segments to maintain the leadership and to make competitors aware that the pricing control can be exercised. The other firms may not be in a position to resist a change and have to follow what the leader does. This pricing technique makes it difficult for new players to enter the markets and also decides the margins to be earned. The markets practicing this is are in an oligopolistic situation thus a healthy competition is not possible. In such a market the new players should be financially sound and have a strong marketing team to plan and implement the strategies related to the launch, distribution, price fluctuation, head on competition etc.

ROOM PRICING TECHNIQUES:

A hotel adopts many pricing modules for arriving at a suitable price for the hotel rooms as it the single largest commodity sold by the hotels. The average sale of room accounts for almost seventy percent of the total revenue generated in the properties except the properties where other activities are given preference.

Rule of Thumb: This simply means that the room prices should be $1 for every $1000 spent on the room for sale to a guest. This approach was adopted to just arrive on an engaging price incase no other parameters are available. But this results in the pricing to be too low in most cases and does not consider the actual expenditures in running a property profitably.

Competitive Pricing: In this type of pricing the existing markets are compared and a lower price is calculated based on the average prices offered by the competing hotels in and around the hotel. This may also overlook the cost input that occurs in construction, finishing and getting the property operational in present conditions. The hotels already in business at the given place would have incurred lower cost as per the time they were constructed thus this difference may lead to lower or no profits for the new hotel.

Market Condition Pricing: In this approach, the management looks at comparable hotels in the geographical market as in competitive pricing to see what they are charging for the same product, but "charge only what the market will accept". A disadvantage of this method is that does not take into consideration the value of the property, and also ignores the results that may be achieved if a strong sales team is utilized to market the hotel.

Hubbart's Formula: This pricing technique was introduced when most the approaches to calculating room pricing were ignoring some or the other aspect of daily operations in a hotel to consider operating costs, desired profits, and expected number of rooms sold (i.e. demand). The method starts with calculating the return on investment before anything else.

The procedure of calculating a room rate is as follows:

1. Calculate the hotel's desired profit by multiplying the desired rate of return (ROI) by the owner's investment.
2. Calculate pre-tax profits by dividing the desired profit by 1 minus hotel's tax rate.
3. Calculate fixed charges and management fees. This calculation includes estimating depreciation, interest expense, property taxes, insurance, amortization, building mortgage, land, rent, and management fees.
4. Calculate undistributed operating expenses. This includes estimating administrative and general expenses, data processing expenses, human resources expenses, transportation expenses, marketing expenses, property operation and maintenance expenses, and energy costs.
5. Estimate non-room operating department income or loss, that is, F&B department income or loss, telephone department income or loss.
6. Calculate the required room department income which is the sum of pre-tax profits, fixed charges and management fees, undistributed operating expenses, and other operating department losses less other department incomes.
7. Determine the rooms' department revenue which is the required room department income, plus other room department direct expenses of payroll and related expenses, plus other direct operating expenses.
8. Calculate the average room rate by dividing rooms' department revenue by the expected number of rooms to be sold.

Food & Beverage Pricing Techniques: The pricing for food and beverages is also done taking into consideration the following:

a. Type of Hotel
b. Type of Restaurant
c. Popularity of the Cuisine
d. Average Covers Sold
e. Wastage and stock required.
f. Menu
g. Ease of availability of raw material
h. Requirement of skilled manpower
a. Standard Recipes
j. Government Regulations relating to food service operations

SUMMARY:

In this unit we have studied about life stages of a product and applied the same to a destination. We have also seen that as per the stage of the destination the marketing strategy of the product is designed. We have also learnt that although the PLC concept is very crucial to identify the life stage of a product but practically most of the manager are not able to apply it theoretically instead they identify the stage of the product life through the features it shows and based on which the managers manipulate their marketing plans. So the concept is not applied by its name but is applied as its features.

We have also learnt that drawing a life cycle curve for a particular product is difficult. We have also studied that the destinations which do not mould their marketing strategies as per the life stage of their destination, fade out from the tourism map. So it is essential to understand the concept of product life cycle and tourism area life cycle and apply them in real life too. In the next block we will study how marketing programs are planned and controlled.

GLOSSARY:

Product life cycle - Product life cycle is the status of a product on time scale from introduction to end in terms of its sales and profits.

Tourism area life cycle - Life cycle as a graphical tool, representing a succession of phases in a normally long period of time, can be a very relevant tool for monitoring several areas of knowledge.

Drifter –these are the most individualistic and least institutionalized tourists. They are the one who usually discover the destination.

Explorer - They like to get off beaten tracks as much as possible. They are early adaptors.

Individual mass tourist –They use the services provided by travel agents to make their arrangements. They prefer to travel in their familiar territory and travel outside it occasionally only.

Organized mass tourist –They always travel with people of their own culture and prefer to travel in groups. They are more interested in sight seeing only and travel locally in air conditioned coaches. They prefer accommodation also in air conditioned hotels with an environment of their origin country. They need an interpreter and do not communicate much with the host community. They like to shop also from the shops where the culture is same as that of their own community.

CHAPTER FOUR

PUBLIC RELATIONS, SALES PROMOTIONS AND INTEGRATED MARKETING COMMUNICATION

INTRODUCTION:

A Marketing Information System (MIS) is a management information system designed to support marketing decision making. Jobber defines it as a "system in which marketing data is formally gathered, stored, analyzed and distributed to managers in accordance with their informational needs on a regular basis." Kotler, et al. (2006) define it more broadly as "people, equipment, and procedures to gather, sort, analyze, evaluate, and distribute needed, timely, and accurate information to marketing decision makers."A formal MIS can be of great benefit to any organization whether profit making or nonprofit making, no matter what its size or the level of managerial finesse. It is true today that in many organizations, MIS is integrated as part of a computerized system. Management Information System (MIS) is an indispensable resource to be carefully managed just like any other resource that the organization may have e.g. human recourses, productive resources, transport resources and financial resources. A marketing information system (MIS) is a set of procedures and methods designed to generate, analyze, disseminate, and store anticipated marketing decision information on a regular, continuous basis. A marketing information system can be used operationally, managerially, and strategically for several aspects of marketing. Some enterprises approach marketing intelligence gathering in a more deliberate fashion and train its sales force, after-sales personnel and district/area managers to take cognizance of competitors‘ actions, customer complaints and requests and distributor problems.

In the previous chapter, you have learnt about distribution channel strategies - nature and importance of distribution systems; channel design decisions, channel management decisions. Every time distribution strategies are to be different in different circumstances to achieve the sales target formulated.

In the present chapter we will be discussing about sales promotion, what are the strategies that are needed to promote sales, how we select, develop implement strategies to increase the sales. Sales promotion is totally different from advertising and personal selling. Sales promotion technique is for short run. On the other hand, advertising is used by any company for long run, while in personal selling, there is personal contact being made by the company to sell the product.

MARKETING INFORMATION AND COMMUNICATION SYSTEM:

To understand the proper role of information systems one must examine what managers do and what information they need for decision making. We must also understand how decisions are made and what kinds of decision problems can be supported by formal information systems. One can then determine whether information systems will be valuable tools and how they should be designed.

We all know that no marketing activity can be carried out in isolation, know when we say it doesn't work in isolation that means there are various forces could be external or internal, controllable or uncontrollable which are working on it. Thus to know which forces are acting on it and its impact the marketer needs to gathering the data through its own resources which in terms of marketing we can say he is trying to gather the market information or form a marketing information system. This collection of information is a continuous process that gathers data from a variety of sources synthesizes it and sends it to those responsible for meeting the market places needs. Depending on a firm's resources and the complexity of its needs, a marketing intelligence network may or may not be fully computerized. The ingredients for a good MIS are consistency, completeness, and orderliness. Marketing plans should be implemented on the basis of information obtained from the intelligence network.

Sources of Marketing Information System

The information needed by marketing managers comes from three main sources:

Internal company information – E.g. sales, orders, customer profiles, stocks, customer service reports etc

Marketing intelligence – This can be information gathered from many sources, including suppliers, customers, and distributors. Marketing intelligence is a term which includes all the everyday information about developments in the market that helps a business prepare and adjust its marketing plans. It is possible to buy intelligence information from outside suppliers (e.g. IDC, ORG, and MARG) who set up data gathering systems to support commercial intelligence products that can be profitably sold to all players in a market.

Market research – Management cannot always wait for information to arrive in bits and pieces from internal sources. Also, sources of market intelligence cannot always be relied upon to provide relevant or up-to-date information (particularly for smaller or niche market segments). In such circumstances, businesses often need to undertake specific studies to support their marketing strategy – this is market research.

Components of a Marketing Information System:

A marketing information system (MIS) is intended to bring together disparate items of data into a coherent body of information. As per Kotler's1 definition says, an MIS is more than a system of data collection or a set of information technologies:"A marketing information system is a continuing and interacting structure of people, equipment and procedures to gather, sort, analyze, evaluate, and distribute pertinent, timely and accurate information for use by marketing decision makers to improve their marketing planning, implementation, and control".

The figure below illustrates the major components of an MIS, the environmental factors monitored by the system and the types of marketing decision which the MIS seeks to underpin.

The explanation of this model of an MIS begins with a description of each of its four main constituent parts: the internal reporting systems, marketing research system, marketing intelligence system and analytical marketing system.

Internal Reporting Systems:

An organization which is working has tremendous amount of information. However, this information often remains under-utilized. Information is usually categorized according to its nature, for example, financial, production, manpower, marketing, stockholding and logistical data. Often the entrepreneur, or various personnel working in the functional departments holding these pieces of data, do not see how it could help decision makers in other functional areas. Similarly, decision makers can fail to appreciate how information from other functional areas might help them and therefore do not request it. The internal records that are of immediate value to marketing decisions are: orders received, stockholdings and sales invoices. These are but a few of the internal records that can be used by marketing managers, but even this small set of records is capable of generating a great deal of information.

Marketing Research System:

Marketing research is a proactive search for information. In many cases, data is collected in a purposeful way to address a well-defined problem (or a problem which can be defined and solved within the course of the study). The other form of marketing research centers not around a specific marketing problem but is an attempt to continuously monitor the marketing environment.

Marketing Intelligence Systems:

Whereas marketing research is focused, market intelligence is not. A marketing intelligence system is a set of procedures and data sources used by marketing managers to shift information from the environment that they can use in their decision making. This scanning of the economic and business environment can be undertaken in a variety of ways. The sources of marketing intelligence can be classified as internal sources vs. external sources. The internal sources to marketing intelligence include company executives, front desk staff, service staff, purchasing agents, and sales force. The external sources of marketing intelligence includes suppliers, convention and tourist bureaus , travel agencies, trade publications, associations, consultants, banks and financial institutions.

Analytical Marketing System:

Within the MIS there has to be the means of interpreting information in order to give direction to decision. These models may be computerized or may not. These mathematical, statistical, econometric and financial models are the analytical subsystem of the MIS.

Functions of Marketing Information System:

The functions of a good MIS can be divided into the following:

Assessing Information Needs– It is important to balance information that managers need against that which they really need and is feasible to obtain. The company must obtain the value of having an item of information against the cost of obtaining it. Since the cost of obtaining, processing, storing and delivering information can add up quickly, managers must carefully identify their real information needs which they think shall add value in decision making.

Developing Information – As discussed earlier information can be obtained through internal databases, marketing intelligence and marketing research. Internal databases usually can be accessed more quickly and cheaply than other information sources, but they also present some problems. It is important to know that every company contains more information than any manager can possibly know or analyze. Today most of the companies are creating data warehouses to store customer data in a single more accessible location. In case of hospitality industry guest information is vital to improve service, create effective advertising and sales promotion programmes, develop new products, improve existing products, develop marketing and sales programmes and in revenue management.

An effective MIS in hospitality industry will collect guest history information, guest information trends. Other sources like guest registration forms, guest comment cards, guest verbal feedback and point of sale information can provide useful insights to design marketing programmes. In addition to internal databases, marketing intelligence can be useful in developing information. The marketing intelligence system aims at developing macro marketing information, competitive information and new innovations and trends. The third source to develop information is conducting market research which is discussed in the next section.

Advantages of Marketing Information System:

Marketing Information System offers many advantages:

1. Organized data collection.
2. A broad perspective.
3. The storage of important data.
4. An avoidance of crises.
5. Coordinated marketing plans.
6. Speed in obtaining sufficient information to make decisions.
7. Data amassed and kept over several time periods.
8. The ability to do a cost-benefit analysis.

The disadvantages of a Marketing information system are high initial time and labor costs and the complexity of setting up an information system. Marketers often complain that they lack enough marketing information or the right kind, or have too much of the wrong kind. The solution is an effective marketing information system.

The Marketing Communications Mix:

The marketing team in a hotel has to design an effective promotion and communication mix for the hotel.

Communication means how we convey our messages to the prospective customers and promotion is the way hotels create the marketing campaigns for the target customers. E.g.

- Brochures& Pamphlets
- Electronic Media Commercials
- Hotel Websites
- Social Media like the Twitter, Facebook, Google, WhatsApp, WeChat, etc.
- Hotel merchandise: Pens, Pencils, Scratch pads and personalized stationery with hotel logo
- Billboards
- GDS, HRS, CRS etc.
- Yearly Events
- CSR Activities

According to David in his book Hospitality Marketing, the objectives of marketing communication can be summarized as follows:

- **Learn**– a new product launch objective for a restaurant opening in September could be: „to generate 15 percent awareness of the restaurant among the target market of ABC1 men and women, within a 15-minute drive-time radius of the site, by the end of October".
- **Feel**– an objective for a conference hotel in an Adriatic tourism destination could be: „to become the destination's conference hotel of first choice for Italian small and medium-sized professional associations within two years".

- **Do–** an objective for a leisure hotel could be: „to generate a 25 percent increase in domestic leisure break Internet bookings in the next twelve-month period".

Marketing Communication or "Marcom" as it is popularly known as is a continuous process with constant inputs using different technologies, internet and individual creativity. The digital formats are readily accessible and can be easily modified to suit the country where the campaign is to be launched. The advantage now a days is that there is information on successful and unsuccessful campaigns to learn from on the internet, thus it is convenient to identify and modify the advertisements and publicity programmes accordingly.

The business communication takes place either on a personal or a non-personal channel. An interaction where the people are communicating one to one is known as personal whereas the interaction where messages are conveyed through other mediums like the advertisements are known as non-personal communication.

Personal communication includes all the communications where people are talking to each other in a formal or informal meeting, over the telephone, using video modes like google, skype, or in a video conference. It may also include personal correspondence through phones, tablets, using the mail or other platforms. The hospitality business has more dependency on personal communication as it is primarily the service oriented industry. The human touch opens up the possibility to directly interact with the guests to understand their requirements on the spot and helps offer the solutions immediately. It is also easier to inform the customer about the complete range of products and services that the hotel has to offer. It also enables the guests to clarify their doubts, convey their choices to the server on duty and to add personal inputs if required. E.g. a guest at the reception may ask for a room on a particular floor or ask the steward to instruct the chef regarding specific taste and spiciness in the ordered dish.

When the hotel uses tent cards, display boards, merchandising tools, magazines, billboards, websites and other such medium to make the potential customers aware of the products and services this is typically a non-personal communication. This definitely reaches out to maximum number of people in a limited time but cannot guarantee the same attention as in personal communication. All such non-personal communication needs to be backed by a very active and creative team or an established agency to which it can be outsourced. The success of non-personal campaigns is dependent on timeliness of launches, accuracy of information, out of the box content, excellent photographic content, and a good storyline created for continuity of the campaign. E.g. the always exciting advertisements of Amul Butter that connect to the day's social and political events.

It is essential for the hospitality businesses to remain in constant touch with their clients irrespective of it being a small or a larger entity. Though in smaller setup it is easy to check and control the communication with their guests as a daily interaction with the owners cannot be ruled out. But in larger properties this role is divided between the heads of the departments and the staff who are in direct contact with the guests.

The 8 P's Of Marketing Mix:

The eight P"s of marketing mix are:

1. Product
2. Place
3. Promotion
4. Price
5. People
6. Packaging
7. Programme
8. Partnership

Product:

Unlike the manufacturing sector where the product is made in the plant and then transported to the customers through various intermediaries the hospitality products and services are created and delivered at the same place, same time and as per the guest demands.

The hotel guests are actively involved in the process of service delivery and sales transaction. E.g. the customers at a fast food outlet or a live kitchen restaurant place their orders and can wait there to see the order being prepared. They are observant of the hygiene, processes, cleanliness of the area, ambience of the outlet and thus feel privileged to have made a good decision to dine there. The guests at the hotel have a higher level of expectations as they are paying for everything that is being given to them. For example the receptionist at the front desk or the server in the restaurant are expected to be professionally dressed and trained in skills to deliver the best under all situations without losing their cool even in stress. The ambience expected by a guest in a five star hotel is beyond what a guest would expect to see in a non-categorized property.

A regular tea drinker working as a commoner on a construction site would be happy to be served the tea in a glass or a kulhad for a price of Rs. 7 to Rs. 10. His expectations are fulfilled with the good strong tea made in the vessel that has been on the fire for the entire day. But in a proper coffee shop a guest who orders a cup of tea expects it to be served separately in a pot and with lot of accompaniments like cookies, milk, cream, sugars, etc. with proper crockery and cutlery as his cost would not be less than Rs.150 – Rs. 250. A compromise would lead to dissatisfaction in quality of service and the server.

Place:

Place is equally important as the product as it represents the location where the product would be sold. The place could be a tangible location or it may also be a virtual location from where the purchase can be initiated and completed after the delivery to a physical location. The hospitality industry has always considered the location as a prime factor with variables like accessibility, ease of travel and natural surrounding taking the lead. A hotel or a dining outlet that cannot be reached easily is usually not on the preferred list of users however exclusive it may be.

Most of the high revenue outlets in food business are strategically located at the busiest junctions and despite the high operating costs they make good profits. The smaller vendors on the highways prefer locations in the outskirts yet closer to the cities but have good parking space for people to get down and shop. The motels on the other hand are located on serene stretches with low settlements around them. A business hotel has to be located in the heart of the city but a resort ideally has to be located in the suburban areas or locations closer to the hills and beaches as the purpose of visit is different from what one has when a city hotel is preferred.

Promotion:

The creation of awareness and making them agree to take a buying decision amongst the prospective customers is promotion. The brand may be well established but if the constant information flow is blocked the buyers tend to go towards the brands that show their presence persistently. The message about the features, specialties, add on benefits are conveyed through advertisements and other merchandising tools. The promotion is done at personal and non-personal levels as per the targeted number of clients. It improves the brand image, brand loyalty and brand positioning in the markets. The tools used have to identified and carefully selected for their advantages and disadvantages.

Price:

The product or services is to be sold for a cost to the buyer thus pricing becomes important decision. The customers look forward to the value for money being paid and is always comparing the prices with other brands offering the similar products. At the same time the company also wishes to earn profits against the sales made thus prices are carefully decided considering the features, benefits and competing brands. The hospitality organizations create the differential in prices of its products and services once they are put in different categories. E.g. A suite room would always be priced above the regular rooms but accordingly the facilities in a suite are comparatively more. The quality of bed sheets in all the star category hotels would be good but the cost and quality of the bed sheet used in a five star property is much better and costly thus leading to an addition to the overall cost of the room. The prices cannot be lower than the cost inputs to prevent losses. There may be times when in highly competitive environment the prices may be slightly above or equal to the breakeven point.

People:

This is a term that is inclusive of the buyers and sellers alike i.e. the guests at a hotel would be happy and satisfied only when the hotel staff puts in their best effort. People need to ensure that the way they are treated and the way they respond to others is ethically correct.

The best of location, best of products and the best of sales promotion may not be able to get good returns if the people representing the organization are not cultured and trained in their respective trades. The hotels that adhere to the standard operating procedures, invest in training and skilling and maintain the quality are favored by any guest and it also ensures the repeat business.

Packaging:

The totality of experience of a guest at a hotel would include satisfaction with the products and services, people, prices, promotions, place or location. Thus, for this guests all the above constitute the packaging of hotel as a product. Similarly in the FMCG markets the way a product is packaged and presented determines how much attention it can grab when it is lying on the shelf. Decently packaged goods with relevant details clearly visible are noticed easily and picked up by the buyers.

Hotels are packaged in terms of ambience, interiors, façade, uniforms of the staff, layout of facilities, presentation of food items, themes of the rooms and restaurants, etc. The intangibility of hospitality sector makes it difficult to convince a client for packaging as an independent variable of marketing mix.

A bakery display unit with beautiful and neatly presented cakes and muffins is what a guest expects when the unit is installed in the lobby of a star hotel. The doorman wearing a crisp and clean uniform receiving a guest at the hotel entrance, the warm welcome of the guests with arti, tika and garland, serving of welcome drink etc. also become a part of packaging.

Programme:

In the hospitality sector programming simply means the itinerary of a trip. A guest plans the visit to a tourist destination well in advance and also takes a decision on the budget to be spent. A good travel agent would thus design the tour package considering the above aspects to ensure that the tourist gets the best in the specified time. The tour operators plan the journey schedules, hotel stays, pickups and drops, meals on the way for the guests to assure that they return satisfied.

Hotels also assist the guests in planning to spend good time inside the hotel by suggesting and informing them about all the facilities, events and special activities being organized. This definitely assures that the guests are happy to come back the next time also.

Ministry of Tourism and State Tourism Boards release the monthly / yearly booklets and directories defining the dates for special events, festivals, trade fairs etc. so that the visitors can plan their visits comfortably. This also helps tourists to identify the destinations and time when the travel would be more fruitful and economical to book compared to the last moment rush. In case of groups checking in at the hotel the tour leader is briefed on the meal timings and outlets where they would be served to make it convenient for all the group members.

Partnership:

The business nowadays works on networking and partnerships at various levels and the one with strong partnerships with sourcing organizations gets the maximum outputs. The hospitality industry has a network of travel intermediaries, ticketing agencies, taxi service operators which constantly provide the bookings for rooms and other services linked to the hotels. This also leads to coordinated efforts to get more business for each of them thereby sharing the profitability with all entities involved in the process. The multipliers effect is visible in tourism sector when a tourist plans a visit to a particular destination. The money that is spent by the tourist is distributed in varying ratios between the accommodation providers, transport modes, dining outlets, banking organizations, the site photographer, souvenir shops at the destinations and many others who are directly or indirectly connected to the activity of tourism.

The ordering in restaurants has moved ahead from manual function to ordering from the tabs that display the picture of the dish along with the prices and specialties on the screen. The tab providers tie up with the restaurants to give a certain percentage of the total number of tabs needed by them to be free along with the software and data backup. The tab companies earn additional revenue by way of ads popping up on the tab while the customers are using them to place orders.

Aviation industry ties up with hotels and other service providers to create loyalty benefits for their frequent flyers. This also passes the advantages to the partner companies. Partnerships with allied services providers in the segment assure addition to revenue and profits but the partners have to be suitable to the business. Like the mileage points collected by a frequent traveler or frequent flyer should be exchangeable with gifts, coupons etc. to be used for other availing other services but this would need a defined partnership with the company that is into the business of manufacturing or trading gift items

Integrated Marketing Communications:

Integrated communication means that the organization is communicating with multiple nationalities at the same time using a single campaign. The basic idea remains same but the authenticity of the message is maintained only when the phrases and words used convey the same meaning as intended. This need core teams with multi lingual experts who are absolutely clear about the vocabulary, taboos, and traditions of a particular language or culture. A marketing communication that resonates with the local culture is easily accepted and becomes popular to yield results.

In the integrated design of a brochure the following are considered:

a. Language Vocabulary: the same words may have different meanings.
b. Copy Space: Some languages take more space in written format.
c. Page Layout requirements as per visual display: The images may have to be adjusted as per text distancing and alignment.
d. Cultural Symbolism: A graphic sign may be symbolic of happiness in some cultures but can be opposite in the other.
e. Color Symbolism: Every culture has its identification of colors thus it is important to respect that while designing.

f. Acceptance in society: Certain images or words may not be acceptable to a community or in a country with respect to the beliefs they have.
g. Government regulations: The age restrictions, content and the time of telecast of a product or service may be bound by these regulations thus may have to be moderated to reach a wider audience.

The hospitality organizations also employ their own teams in marketing and sales apart from the employees in the front desk, reservations and all those at the point of sales. The reservation manager and the sales teams have to visit the clients outside the hotel premises also to ensure proper connect and assurance of business from them. The liaison role has gained importance in today's marketing as most of the hotels now follow this practice. The more one is directly or indirectly connected to the market, more shall be return in terms of sales. The marketing communication offices may be set outside the hotel locally, regionally or internationally depending on the quantum of business necessary for profitability of the business. The hotels may also get into tie ups and agreements for generating sales through partners.

The concept of integrated marketing communications is the response to this confused approach to organizing the international marketing communication function.

The hotels and hospitality firms can be identified by their unique signage and standardized layouts of printed medium, by their specific colors e.g. Kwality Walls India in Red and White and Baskin Robbins with White, Pink and Blue signage.

It is good idea to run paid adverts in the leading dailies and popular magazines which generate interest of the potential customers and also make the existing customers aware of the new additions in terms of products, services and locations. The communication has to economical and any changes or modifications should be approved by the persons in charge of the marketing campaigns.

Following are some of the communications channels to convey the firm's messages and promotions to the prospective consumers:

- **Print**
- **Personal Selling**
- **The Corporate Sales Team**

Print:

Print Medium: A hospitality organization or a hotel has significant range of printed material also termed as collateral. All the communication between the guests and the hotel takes place via various forms and formats e.g. reservation and registrations forms, bills and invoices, receipts and stationery in the rooms etc.

Print material for individual hospitality units includes:

- Stationery
- Hotel brochures, tariff and price lists
- Restaurant menus and wine lists
- Conference brochures
- Wedding brochures
- Function prospectus
- Promotional material for the sales team
- In-room information (hotel facilities and in room service menus)

- Special product brochures (for example, treasure hunt weekends)
- Special price promotional flyers
- Newsletters.
- Tent Cards
- Personalized stationery for the guests.

Print material for Chain Hotels:

- Corporate directory listing all branded hotels in the country, region or world
- Corporate leisure breaks brochure
- Corporate conference brochure
- Group business brochure targeting tour operators
- Corporate sales team promotional material
- Corporate newsletters
- Loyalty club leaflets, application forms and newsletters
- Special promotions.

Personal Selling:

This is direct communication technique used to deliver relevant information about the hotel to the target markets. Although it consists of telemarketing, mails and messages but the main focus in hospitality is face-to-face contact with potential clients by the sales team members. The team's members have to travel in and outside the city, thus have recurring expenditure and continued exertion. This adds extra costs to the overall budgeted expenditure if the number of trips increases but the expected result is not seen. Hotel staffs are always playing this role of sales personnel by being attentive to the guest needs and demands.

Bulk bookings for conferences, meetings, dealer meets, seminars and workshops, residential conferences etc. are all possible only through personal selling. This is because the client can clearly put across the demands and hotel sales person can clarify any issues at the same time. This bookings can't be discussed over the phone or over the emails as there are many issues that get sorted out in a face to face interaction esp. price negotiations and menu changes.

Personal selling is useful in the following conditions:

a. A detailed explanation is needed if the package has many constituents.
b. When the perceived value of the sales and revenue earned is noticeably high.
c. The product specification can be adapted to suit the needs of the client
d. It is known that the prospective client engages in lot of negotiations and bargaining.
e. The prospective clients, or intermediaries, can influence or make the decision to book business.
f. A sales person visiting the potential customer is expected.
g. When the competitors can influence or take away the deals.

<u>The Corporate Sales Team:</u>

The Corporate Sales Team: This refers to the set of people who form the core team for hotel sales and marketing. All the "Key Accounts" i.e. the organizations that give maximum business to the hotel are identified and the sales team assures regular communication with them by way of personalized visits, phone calls and sending mails on important occasions. The sales team follows standard steps to assure business from key accounts and new clients. They may be as follows:

a. **Prospecting:** As the term suggest it refers to the search for potential consumers from local companies, finding existing and the customers who were using the hotel services earlier but have stopped now, from the hotel's guest history. It is also seen that these leads shall be ready to purchase the present range of services and are in a position to pay the revised prices.
b. **Sales calls:** The hotel sales executives visit the prospective customer's office following the Cold Call i.e. without prior appointment but it not as effective as a pre-booked sales call to save time and effort for both the sales agent and more importantly the clients. This may have to be repeated to assure the client build confidence in the person and the products being offered. The person is also responsible to arrange the meetings between the clients and his senior team members if called for.
c. **Sales Blitz**: This means that the entire team works together in a specific location for a defined period and consolidates the business. The team may make use of all the methods like taking appointments, surprise visits, cold calls and tele - marketing at the same time.
d. **Familiarization Visits**: The hotel sales team members have to coordinate with the hotel in case a prospective customer wishes to visit the hotel before finalizing the future business with the property. They should be in touch with the respective department heads to assure the visit is fruitful by sharing complete information about the needs of the visiting client.

e. **Advertising:** Advertisements are mass communication channels through which the organizations reaches out to fairly large number of clients and prospective customers in one go. But the assurance of response in terms of buying that advertised product or service is never clear till the time the person contacts the hotel for business. This is expensive compared to other mediums as the cost is higher and can be used only once. Also, the effectiveness cannot be measured in real time.

The advertisement media used is choice of the company but the advertiser is bound by legal, voluntary and social constraints that advertisers need to recognize. Most countries have legal restrictions on advertising, like censorship for content in the advertisement designed to ensure that that dishonest claims and misleading information is not circulated.

The following media can be used for advertising campaigns:

- Daily and Weekly Newspapers
- Magazines
- Government Publications
- Tourism board Publications
- Broadcast media (radio, cable television, internet, etc.)
- Social Media.
- Banners or pop-ups on search engines, directories and websites
- Billboards and posters
- Ambient media (buses, taxis, trains, gas and petrol stations)
- Signage for government buildings

- Signage at highways and expressways.

a. **Newspapers:** The cost depends on the following factors:

    - Circulation and readership – the number of copies sold and the number of readers per copy
    - Geographic coverage – local, regional, national

- Audience profile – social grade, income and lifestyle
- Size– bigger adverts cost more; display adverts can use graphics such as line drawings or photographs, whilst classified advertising is copy only
- Page / Location of advert – where an advert is actually placed in the newspaper (front page, back page and requests for a specific spot are more expensive)
- Days – Sunday is one of the most popular days to read the newspapers, and so it is more expensive
- Number – a series of adverts booked at the same time can qualify for volume discounts.

b. **Magazines:** The cost factors are similar to the newspapers but the magazines are usually theme or subject based thus have a defined readership linked to the same interest. An adventure resort putting an advertisement in a business magazine would not yield results as compared to its placement in a magazine which deals with youth affairs. The advantage is that these can be stored for longer periods or at least till the next issue is circulated.
c. **Government Publications:** E newsletters, magazines, digital books etc. are published by the Ministry of Tourism, GOI to update the masses about the changes and growth in the hospitality and tourism industry.

d. **Local Tourism Board / Tour Operators Publications:** Yellow pages can be categorized as a tourist board publication as it carries advertisements for and listings of accommodation, attractions, bars and restaurants, and events taking place in the area. Potential visitors to the area contact the destination marketing organization to request information, and are sent these brochures. For smaller accommodation businesses, for example a farmhouse with bed and breakfast, Tourist Board publications provide one of the most effective promotional tools.

e. **Broadcast Media**: There was a time when the television had maximum audience, and was consequently the most expensive advertising medium. The introduction of web based applications and mobile phones have cut down on this. This is still a costly medium as the prime time slots are still the most expensive as at this time the medium has maximum number of viewers. FM Radio is the latest addition to the broadcast medium which has greater audience. The youngsters follow the RJs for respective shows and respond to the advertisements too.

The introduction of satellite television shopping channels has created new opportunities for companies to promote hospitality, travel and tourism products. Travel agents like Thomas Cook have developed their own dedicated interactive television channels, which promote package holidays, cruises and destinations that can be booked by viewers as they watch the programs.

f. **Malls and Multiplexes:** It is similar to television advertising but is relatively cheaper. Since they attract a younger audience; the fast-food chains, local restaurants, health and gym operators, adventure sports or water sports / theme parks ads can be seen here.

g. **Signage:** The organizations have now started putting up important and informative signage for the government institutions with the logo of their own. The concept of green and clean cities displayed on kiosk boards or the ones that ask the common citizens to obey the traffic rules are visible on the main roads and highways but are sponsored by a particular brand that can appropriately be noticed along with this information.

h. **Ambient Media**: Many hospitality brands and state tourism boards are making good use of the public transport systems to display their advertisements. The recent being major tourist trains in India and the state roadways using this medium to promote themselves.

i. **Merchandising:** This means of communication is used by the hotels to communicate with the guests who visit the hotels, the resident guests and guests who come for dining or use of membership facilities at the hotel. It isa short term inducement to motivate an immediate purchase of a product or service. Merchandising is done either to introduce a new product to the market or to boost sales of existing product. The sales promotion includes offering discount coupons, contests and sweepstakes, free samples, and premiums. In the hotel industry, a "buy three get one free" offer for dining at a hotel for dinner buffet is an example. Some hotels have the "Happy Hour Drink Buffet" where diners can enjoy the all-you-can-drink beverages for a special price. This is usually effective in creating excitement about products among the guests. Similarly, restaurants may offer "early bird" special to senior citizens if they have their dinner before 7:00 p.m. so to generate business during slow meal period. The hotel may offer special discounts on its facilities if the customer pays with a partner bank's credit card.Merchandising is the in-house display which is used to encourage the sales for the organization or the brand. E.g. Starbucks uses the merchandising technique to sell the coffee beans, coffee mugs and coffee machines in their stores, rather than just selling freshly brew coffee.

The POS (Point of Sales): All the areas where the guests directly interact with the hotel staff for purchase of hotel's products or services are known as point of sale in a hotel. The staff on duty plays the dual role or server and the sales promoter as he /she can induce short-term or immediate sales. These are also the contact points where in-house promotions are displayed and can be discussed with the hotel guests freely.

Hotels and dining outlets use a variety of point-of-sale material to promote in-house products. These may be the menus, leaflets, coupons and posters at the reception desk and in the lift, bedrooms, bars and restaurants, and at leisure outlets. It is usually a tangible piece of collateral material that is easily noticed by the customers and assists in improving the image of the entity. But POS materials should be checked for the dates and schedules as the ones with outdated information sends a wrong message.

Souvenirs and takeaways: Hotels are now coming up with souvenirs and take away stationery products that keep the information and memories of the hotel alive with the guests. Personalized pens with guest names are kept in rooms of higher categories and when a special gathering is arranged like a residential get-together or conference.

Hospitality Sales Promotion: Hospitality organizations run the sales and marketing campaigns for assuring their presence in the markets and its segments from where the business is sourced. It is necessary as the number of new brands and sub brands in the industry is increasing in manifolds. New players are entering the markets with entirely different gamut of products and services. The menus are going under sea change, the facilities like attached multiplexes and shopping arenas, brand stores, day care facilities for children and infants, gaming zones with real and virtual gaming facilities etc. which were unheard of in earlier days. Festival celebrations and themed events have become common in all the cities and hotels take a lead in organizing and hosting such activities irrespective of the category and brand. Therefore the promotional campaigns have to be strong enough to attract maximum customers to be a part of these events.

A successful campaign is assured when the sales and marketing team plans the activities and event promotion in collaboration with the departments in the hotel that would be integral in making it a success. It should look into the existing customer base and then decide the number of events and prices in a season. It is essential to check the promotional activities being done by the competitors so that a difference is crafted and made visible to the public. Discounts and packages should be planned as per budgeted expenditure and facilities to be extended during the event. The effort has to be at par with the brand image and the position a hospitality firm holds in the market. The activities have also to be creative and attention grabbing so that it gets quicker publicity and approval from the targeted customers. The selection of media for taking this campaign to the market is also important e.g. an event targeted for youth has to be marketed through social media, internet and preferably a dedicated app for the event. The duration of promotional campaigns has to be appropriate to attract the attention but not too long that the interest is lost in waiting.

Examples:

- Meal plans like CP, MAP, and AP that considerably reduce the actual room prices.
- Price discounts on accommodation, food, drink and leisure activities in holiday packages.
- Added value promotions – bundling a range of hospitality products into a single price and package.
- Discount vouchers and coupons.
- Frequent Traveler Programs.
- Festive discounts on meals and events.
- Sightseeing and theme dinners included in suite packages for leisure traveler.

SALES PROMOTION:

In the current scenario, every businessman wants to increase the sale of goods that he is dealing in. He can use one of the several ways for that purpose. One might have heard about "win a tour to Europe/Australia etc", "crorepati bano", "50% extra on purchase of 2 kg products", "scratch and win a prize" etc. You might also have seen getting surprise gifts like lunch box, pencil box, pen, shampoo pouch etc. offered free with products.

There are other offers, like in exchange of existing model of mobile/fridge/washing machine etc, you can get a new model at a reduced price. You may have also observed in your neighboring markets notices of "winter sale", "summer sale", "trade fairs" "Diwali offers" , "discount up to 70%" and many other schemes to attract customers to buy certain products. All these are incentives offered by manufacturers or dealers to increase the sale of their goods. These incentives may be in the form of free samples, gifts, discount coupons, demonstrations, shows, contests etc. All these measures normally motivate the customers to buy more and thus, it increases sales of the product. This approach of selling goods is known as "Sales Promotion".

Sales promotion does not include advertising, personal selling and publicity that help to increase sales through non- repetitive and one time communication. In other words, it includes marketing activities other than personal selling, advertising and publicity that stimulate consumer purchasing and dealer effectiveness, such as point of purchase displays, shows and exhibitions, demonstrations and various non-recurring selling efforts not in the regular routine. Sales promotion adopts short term, non-recurring techniques to increase the sales in different ways. These offers are not available to the customers throughout the year. During festivals, end of the seasons, year ending and some other occasion, these schemes are generally available in the market.

Therefore, sales promotion consists of all activities other than advertising and personal selling that help to increase sales of a particular product or commodity. Sales promotion, a key ingredient in many marketing campaigns, consists of a diverse collection of incentive tools, mostly short term, designed to stimulate trial or quicker or greater purchase of particular products or services by consumers or the trade. Whereas advertising offers a reason to buy, sales promotion offers an incentive to buy.

Sales promotion includes tools for consumer promotion (samples, coupons, cash refund offers, prices off, premiums, prizes, patronage rewards, free trials, warranties, tie-in promotions, cross-promotions, point-of-purchase displays and demonstrations); trade promotion (prices off, advertising and display allowances and free goods) and business and sales force promotion (trade shows and conventions, contests for sales representatives and specialty advertising). In years past, the advertising-to-sales- promotion ratio was about 60:40. Today, in many consumer-packaged-goods companies, sales promotion accounts for 65–75 percent of the overall promotional budget. Several factors have contributed to this trend; particularly in consumer markets. Internal factors include the following: Promotion is now more accepted by top management as an effective sales tool, more product managers are qualified to use sales-promotion tools and product managers are under greater pressure to increase current sales. External factors include: The number of brands has increased, competitors use promotions frequently, many brands are seen as being similar, consumers are more price-oriented, the trade demands more deals from manufacturers and advertising efficiency has declined because of rising costs, media clutter and legal restraints.

Sales promotion has been defined as under: According to **Philip Kotler**, "those marketing activities other than personal selling, advertising and publicity that stimulate consumer purchasing and dealer effectiveness, such as display, shows, demonstrations, expositions and various other non-current selling efforts, not in ordinary routine."

In the words of **Robert C. and Scott A.**, "Sales promotion consists of a diverse collection of incentive tools, mostly short- term, designed to stimulate quicker and/or greater purchase of particular products/services by consumers or trade."

According to **Harold Whitehead**, "Sales promotion includes the dissemination of information to wholesalers, retailers, customers (actual and potential) and to the salesman".

In the words of **Boone and Kurtz**, "Sales promotion can be defined as those forms of promotion other than advertising and personal selling that increase sales through non- recurrent selling efforts".

In the words of **McCarthy**, "Sales promotion is any method of informing persuading or reminding consumers, wholesalers, retailers about the marketing mix of product, place and price which has been assembled by the marketing manager".

According to **American Marketing Association**, "Those marketing activities other than personal selling, advertising and publicity that stimulate consumer purchasing and dealer effectiveness such as displays, shows and exposition, demonstration and various non-recurrent selling, not in the ordinary routine."

In the words of **L.K. Johnson**, "Sales promotion consists of all those activities whose purpose is to supplement, to co-ordinate and to make more effective efforts of the sales force, of the advertising department and of the distributors; and to increase sales and otherwise stimulate consumers to take greater initiative in buying." After going through above definition, you can now summarize that sales promotion is a very important tool of marketing which includes samples, coupons, cash refund offers, prices off etc. So, sales promotion refers to irregular and personal sales (leaving advertising and publicity) and all the marketing activities which stimulate the consumers to purchase more and the traders to increase their sales like decoration, fairs, exhibitions, displays etc.

Objectives of Sales Promotion:

Sales promotion tools vary in their specific objectives. A free sample stimulates consumer trial while a free management advisory service cements a long-term relationship with a retailer.

From the marketer's perspective, sales promotion serves three essential roles it informs, persuades and reminds prospective and current customers and other selected audiences about a company and its products. The relative importance of those roles varies according to the circumstances faced by a firm. The most useful product or brand will be a failure if no one knows it is available. Because distribution channels are often long, a product may pass through many lands between a producer and consumers. Therefore, a producer must inform middlemen as well as the ultimate consumers or business users about the product. Wholesalers, in turn must inform retailers and retailers must inform consumers. As the number of potential customers grows and the geographic dimensions of a market expand, the problems and costs of informing the market increase.

Another purpose of sales promotion is persuasion. The intense competition among different industries puts tremendous pressure on the promotional programmes of sellers. In India, even a product designed to satisfy a basic physiological need requires strong persuasive promotion because consumers have many alternatives to choose from. In the case of luxury product, for which sales depend on the ability to convince consumers that the products benefits exceed those of other luxuries, persuasion is even more important.

Consumers also must be reminded about a product's availability and its potential to satisfy. Sellers bombard the market place units, hundreds of messages every day in the hope of attracting new consumers and establishing markets for new products. Given the intense competition for consumers" attention even an established firm must constantly remind people about its brand to retain a place in their minds. Much of a firm's sales promotion may be intended simply to offset competitors marketing activity by keeping its brand in front of the market.

After having discussion on sales promotion, you must have learnt that the main objective of sales promotion is to increase sales. However, there are few other objectives of sales promotion. The objectives are:

- Introduction of new products
- Attract new customers and retaining existing ones
- Maintaining sales of seasonal products
- Meeting the challenge with competitors
- To increase sales in off season
- To increase the inventories of business buyers Let us have a brief discussion about these objectives.

Introduction of New Products:

Have you ever heard about distribution of free samples? Perhaps you know that many companies distribute free samples while introducing new products. The consumers after using these free samples may develop a taste for it and buy the products later for consumption.

Attracting New Customers and Retaining Existing Ones:

Sales promotion measures help to attract or create new customers for the product. While moving in the market, customers are generally attracted towards the product that offers discount, gift, prize, etc. These are some of the tools used to encourage the customers to buy the goods. Thus, it helps to retain the existing customers and at the same time it also attracts some new customers to buy the product.

Maintaining Sales of Seasonal Products:

There are some products like air conditioner, fan, refrigerator, cooler, winter clothes, room heater, sunscreen lotion, glycerin soap etc. which are used only in a particular season. To maintain the sales of these types of products, normally the manufacturers and dealers give off-season discount. For example, you can buy air conditioner in winter at a reduced price. Similarly you may get discount on winter clothes during summer.

Meeting the challenge with competitors:

Today's business faces competition all the time. New products frequently come to the market and at the same time improvement also takes place. So, sales promotion measures have become essential to retain the market share of the seller or producer in the product market.

To increase sales in off season:

Buyers may be encouraged to use the product in off seasons by showing them the variety of uses of the product.

To increase the inventories of business buyers:

Retailers may be induced to keep in stock more units of a product so that more sales can be affected.

Tools of Sales Promotion:

To increase the sale of any product, manufactures or producers adopt various techniques like sample, gift, bonus and many more. These are known as tools or techniques or methods of sales promotion. Let us know more about some of the commonly used tools of sales promotion.

Free samples

You might have received free samples of shampoo, washing powder, coffee powder, etc. while purchasing various items from the market. Sometimes these free samples are also distributed by the shopkeeper even without purchasing any item from his shop. These are distributed to attract consumers to try out a new product and thereby create new customers. Some businessmen distribute samples among selected persons in order to popularize the product. For example, in the case of medicine free samples are distributed among physicians, in the case of textbooks, specimen copies are distributed among teachers.

Premium or Bonus offer

A milk shaker along with Nescafe, mug with Bournvita, toothbrush with 500 grams of toothpaste, 30% extra in a pack of one kilogram are the examples of premium or bonus given free with the purchase of a product. They are effective in inducing consumers to buy a particular product. This is also useful for encouraging and rewarding existing customers.

Exchange schemes

It refers to offering exchange of old product for a new product at a price less than the original price of the product. This is useful for drawing attention to product improvement. „Bring your old mixer-cum-juicer and exchange it for a new one just by paying Rs.500" or „exchange your black and white television with a color television" are various popular examples of exchange scheme.

Price-off offer

Under this offer, products are sold at a price lower than the original price. „Rs. 2 off on purchase of Dove soap, Rs. 16 off on a pack of 250 grams of Taj Mahal tea, Rs. 1000 off on Cell phone" etc. are some of the common schemes. This type of scheme is designed to boost up sales in off-season and sometimes while introducing a new product in the market.

Coupons

Sometimes, coupons are issued by manufacturers either in the packet of a product or through an advertisement printed in the newspaper or magazine or through mail. These coupons can be presented to the retailer while buying the product. The holder of the coupon gets the product at a discount. For example, you might have come across coupons like, „show this and get Rs. 16 off on purchase of 5 kg. of Annapurna Atta". The reduced price under this scheme attracts the attention of the prospective customers towards new or improved products.

Fairs and Exhibitions

Fairs and exhibitions may be organized at local, regional, national or international level to introduce new products, demonstrate the products and to explain special features and usefulness of the products. Goods are displayed and demonstrated and their sale is also conducted at a reasonable discount. 'International Trade Fair' at Pragati Maidan which is held from 14th to 27th November every year is a well known example of Fairs and Exhibitions as a tool of sales promotion.

Trading stamps

In case of some specific products, trading stamps are distributed among the customers according to the value of their purchase. The customers are required to collect these stamps of sufficient value within a particular period in order to avail of some benefits. This tool induces customers to buy that product more frequently to collect the stamps of required value.

Scratch and win offer

To induce the customer to buy a particular product, „scratch and win" scheme is also offered. Under this scheme, a customer scratches a specific marked area on the package of the product and gets the benefit according to the message written there. In this way, customers may get some item free as mentioned on the marked area or may avail of price-off or sometimes visit different places on special tour arranged by the manufacturers.

Money Back offer

Under this scheme, customers are given assurance that full value of the product will be returned to them if they are not satisfied after using the product. This creates confidence among the customers with regard to the quality of the product. This technique is particularly useful while introducing new products in the market.

Developing Sales Promotion Strategies:

A sales promotion is frequently used by a business to increase sales of a specific product or service. Successful sales promotions draw new customers as well as keeping current customers. There are three sales promotion strategies: A "push strategy" pushes products through the distribution chain with the in-store consumer as the final link. Discounts and free trials are two examples of "push strategy" sales promotion tools.

In contrast to the "push strategy," the "pull strategy" focuses on stimulating the consumer to purchase the product directly from the manufacturer. Cash refunds and loyalty programs are two examples of "pull strategies." The third strategy is a combination of the first two and may offer a consumer incentive in addition to a dealer discount.

Instructions Developing Sales Promotion Strategies:

List Your Product's Attributes: Focus on the features that make your product different from similar products. Here are some examples: Your product possesses a specific benefit that competing products lack; your product comes in a popular larger size or your product has just been praised by a major celebrity. All of these positive qualities can be used to promote and increase sales of your product.

Examine Your Target Market: Identify those consumer groups likely to use your product. Depending on the product, you may have one target market (example: ladies' handbags); or you could have several markets (example: hiking boots with built-in antimicrobial insoles).List non-traditional markets that can also benefit from your product.

Analyze Your Competitors' Tactics: Before you can "pull away from the pack," you need to see where the pack is running. Look at local advertisements, point of purchase offers and other promotional tactics, your competition is using to sell similar products. If possible, make a few anonymous visits to gauge the product's sales for yourself.

Develop A "Win-Win" Sales Promotion: Using the information, you have gathered about your product, market and competitors; develop a sales promotion that benefits both the retailer and the customer. Here are two examples: Develop a customer loyalty card program with a truly exceptional reward for completing the loyalty card (e.g., a certificate for a free massage from a health product manufacturer). Another "win-win" sales promotion may offer a complete bicyclist clothing package with the purchase of a higher end bicycle.

Inform And Enthuse Your Employees: A key element of a successful sales promotion is the contagious attitude of employees towards the product. If they use and love the product, they will be happy to communicate that value to the customers.

Conduct An Interactive Training Session About The Product: Provide a sample for all employees; if that's not feasible, ensure that everyone has time to try or study the product. Talk about the product's benefits for consumers and highlight the product's outstanding value when compared with similar products. Make the session fun and conclude it with a great prize for the winner of a product trivia contest.

Develop Criteria For The Promotion's Success: Before you implement the sales promotion, identify a quantitative measure of its success. This achievement might come in the form of higher sales dollars, new customers signed up for a long-term service plan or other objective criteria.

Implement The Promotion: First, ensure that you have plenty of the targeted products on hand. Next, highlight the product (and the promotional enticement) with store graphics and promotional supplies provided by the manufacturer. Make sure the product's benefits are communicated by the displays and by your employees. One unconventional tactic is to hire an outgoing costumed version of the product, station her in the parking lot and task her with waving customers into the store. To reach your target markets, put your advertising message into the media utilized by these markets. Here are two examples: For a golf product, advertise on golf websites, in regional golf publications and at local country clubs. For organic makeup products and cosmetics, advertise in organic and health magazines and at health and fitness centers.

Importance of Sales Promotion:

The importance of sales promotion in modern marketing has increased mainly on account of its ability in promoting sales and preparing the ground for future expansion. The main objective of sales promotion is to attract the prospective buyer towards the product and induce him to by the product at the point of purchase. At the salesman's level, its objective is to achieve more sales. At the retailer's level, the purpose is to sell a particular product of a manufacturer. At the consumer's level, the main idea is to enable the consumer to buy more of a product more frequently and also to introduce new uses for the product. Thus, it is a "catch-all" method and is used as an effective tool of marketing.

From the Point of View of Manufacturers:

Sales promotion is important for manufacturers because:

- It helps to increase sales in a competitive market and thus increases profits
- It helps to introduce new products in the market by drawing the attention of potential customers

- When a new product is introduced or there is a change of fashion or taste of consumers, existing stocks can be quickly disposed of.
- It stabilizes sales volume by keeping its customers with them. In the age of competition, it is quite much possible that a customer may change his/her mind and try other brands. Various incentives under sales promotion schemes help to retain the customers.

From the Point of View of Consumers:
Sales promotion is important for consumers because:

- The consumer gets the product at a cheaper rate
- It gives financial benefit to the customers by way of providing prizes and sending them to visit different places
- The consumer gets all information about the quality, features and uses of different products
- Certain schemes like money back offer creates confidence in the mind of customers about the quality of goods; and
- It helps to raise the standard of living of people. By exchanging their old items, they can use latest items available in the market. Use of such goods improves their image in society.

Functions of Sales Promotion:

Various functions of sales promotions are explained briefly:

Low cost: Sales Promotion is always the outcome of large-scale production. Large- scale production itself is meant for low cost. But this could be achieved only with appropriate methods of large-scale selling. Ultimately, therefore, sales promotion assures of a low cost.

Effective sales support: Basically, sales promotion policies, supplement the efforts of personal and impersonal salesmanship (Advertising). It is found that good sales promotion materials make the salesman's effort more productive. The activities reduce his time spent in prospecting and reduce the turndowns.

Increased speed of product acceptance: Most of the sales promotion devices (contests, coupons, etc) can be used faster than the other promotion methods such as advertisement.

Better control: The management has effective control over the various methods used and in its effectiveness. The financial aspects also could be sales promotion and could be compared with the profit per unit of the product sold.

Reasons for Increasing Use of Sales Promotion:

Sales promotion activities have become increasingly popular among business firms due to the following factors:

Brand proliferation: As companies are increasingly using branding to identify a product from competing products the number of brands has increased tremendously. Brands become less distinctive and product features cannot be advertised very effectively. Companies adopt sales promotion to ensure their share of the limited space with the retailers.

Trade pressure: There is now greater pressure on manufacturers to provide support and allowances due to the growth of super market, chain assist retailers and thereby secure their cooperation.

Growth competition: When one manufacturer adopts aggressive promotional strategy to create a brand image, the sales of other manufacturers are affected. In order to maintain their sales, other manufacturers also start sales promotion activities leading to virtually a promotion war.

Recession: During a recession, consumers can be persuaded to wait as during recession, business comes to zero. Therefore, manufacturers make use of these activities to reduce inventory and to improve cash position.

Quick returns: Sales promotion activities are launched quickly and yield faster. These activities also motivate the over burdened and lethargic sales force. Therefore, there is wide spread use of sales promotion schemes.

Competent staff: Due to specialization, new staff positions have created in several companies. Executives with specialized qualifications have greater faith in modern techniques of sales promotion.

Change in attitudes: Earlier, senior managements were of the view that sales promotion spoiled the image of their brand. But the success of competitors in sales promotion has made sales promotion more acceptable to such managements.

Limitation of Sales Promotion:

To improve the public image of the firm sales promotion, however, suffers from the following limitations:

1. There is a feeling that such seasonal sales promotional activities are mainly intended to sell an inadequate product.
2. The second criticism is that such discounts are not real, since the prices of the products are already inflated.
3. These activities are short lived, so the results realized are also short-lived. As soon as these concessions are withdrawn, the demand also falls.
4. It is a short-run tool used to stimulate immediate increase in demand.
5. The producer provides the information regarding quality, uses, different uses of products and its price etc, to the consumers while introducing their products.
6. Sales promotion is also helpful in increasing the number of new customers. The producers give the customers different concessions such as: purchase two and get one as "free".
7. For sales promotion, advertisements are given to the leading magazines which ultimately result in more goodwill of the company.
8. The main purpose of sales promotion is to increase the sales of the product of the company. Promotional activities like free gifts induce the customers to purchase. Thus, sales increase.
9. One of the objectives of the sales promotion is to keep the memory of the product alive in the minds of the present customers.
10. The intensive competition has necessitated the sales promotional activities to educate their customers.
11. Most of the sales promotion devices (such as contents, premium coupons etc) can be used faster than the other methods such as advertisements.

PUBLIC RELATIONS:

Public relation is the day to day interaction of an organization with its existing and potential clients. It is aimed at building a good social image of the organization and to gain publicity in the area. It is carefully monitored by Public Relation Officers especially appointed for the purpose as they are trained in giving statements on behalf of the company and also represent the company at various social and media platforms. The PR professionals are responsible to form a positive and favorable business environment for the organization by assuring timely media coverage of events and CSR activities. Hotels and hospitality organizations generally have these PR Managers in the regional or national offices to keep an open channel of communication with the government officials, representatives of trade bodies, and in some cases the stakeholders also.

According to Grunig's Excellence Theory, PR is the process of ensuring that decisions made by organizations are mutually beneficial between the organization itself and its audiences. This means using strategic communication to negotiate with your audience, resolve conflicts, and promote mutual understandings all backed with thorough research. This type of system is put in motion when generating a strategic PR Plan.

PR Planning may be done using either the R.P.I.E (Research – Planning – Implementation- Evaluation) model or R.A.C.E (Research – Action & Planning – Communication & Relationship Building – Evaluation) model.

Features of a good PR exercise:

1. It should generate positive publicity.
2. It should be in line with the brand image of the company.
3. It should help the brand consolidate its positioning in the markets.
4. Creative in nature to attract the attention of prospective customers and the media.
5. It should be simple and easily understandable by all relevant sectors.
6. The information presented to the outside media and press should be professionally designed and circulated with all the supporting information, photographs, etc.
7. Press release should be well articulated and sent on official documents verified by the senior management.
8. Familiarization visits should be planned in consultation with other departments so that the visitors are received and treated professionally.
9. News about the success stories, awards and accolades won, appreciation by social organizations, launch of new sub brands, food outlets, events and activities should be timely and regularly shared with media and on the hotel websites.
10. Internet and app based publicity should be promoted.
11. CSR activities should be done in liaison with the local government bodies and social organizations so that they may be effective and also get covered.
12. It should forge mutually beneficial and strong relationships with all concerned entities whether publics or government.

Race Model of Public Relations Planning:

This begins with understanding of the roles and responsibilities of the internal and external customers who are connected to the business. We should be able to assess the purpose of existence of the company i.e. why has it come into the particular business segment, who are the people who get affected by it, and what does the organization has to offer to the stakeholders. The research could be formal or informal or a combination of both to identify what is being done, how is being done and what improvements can be brought in for better publicity. All information should be collected systematically so that it is easier to process and results can be assimilated without delay.

Action & Planning: This is the stage when we develop policies and strategies and prepare an action plan to start working on the findings obtained in the research process. Dr. Hongmei Shen, PR author and researcher, recommends using S.M.A.R.T. objectives to set goals for a program based on research and analysis. Shen recommends having a:Specific (purpose)Measurable (outcomes)Attainable (objective)Realistic (goal)Time (available and necessary)

SMART objective model assures that the organization sets attainable goals keeping in view the capabilities and strengths of individuals who form the PR team. It also helps in measuring the achievements for better evaluation and modifications if required.

Communication & Relationship Building: An organization has the opportunity to develop trustworthy and mutually beneficial relationships with its clients by being transparent and honest to them. The communication should be continuous for regular sharing of information with the stakeholders and whenever necessary the meetings may be scheduled to clarify doubts; if any. A two way communication must be encouraged to assure them of fair trade practices and faithful offering.

Evaluation: This is continuous process that follows the implementation and action phase. Here the organization examines and evaluates the effectiveness of the PR campaign. It also measures the performance against the objectives set earlier and monitors the additional steps to be taken for the future. It should be an ongoing process that is measured against your previously set goals to analyze overall effectiveness. The success of the campaign can also be measured by studying the Secondary Data, Case Studies, Press Clippings (How much coverage was generated Advertising Value Equivalent – Editorial coverage value (Column length/air time x Ad rate), Media Content Analysis (Tracking past and future success and failure), Readability Test – Years of education required to understand campaign, Audience and reader surveys Focus groups and interviews.

PR and Destination Marketing: Destination marketing is being supported by public relation activities as they can promote the destinations if some special activity is organized there on regular intervals or it is an important destination for conduct of social and cultural events. The destinations where movies are shot, the popular shows are screened can be promoted through PR campaigns attracting more people to come and experience them. The inherent desire to be the part of history, to visit featured places are common now and people are willing to travel to these exclusive destinations.

Direct Marketing:

When a product or service is sold to a customer without the involvement of intermediaries or middlemen it is direct marketing. A travel enthusiast who is also an avid user of

Facebook may decide to purchase an adventure trip just by seeing the pop up ad while surfing through his account. Whenever the companies communicate with the clients directly via the mediums like telephone, text messages, mails, personal meetings it is part of direct marketing. This is beneficial to both the parties as it reduces the cost for the purchaser and increases the margins of seller as the commissions are not to be paid to the middlemen. This method is also beneficial to the producer of goods as the companies may purchase from them at better prices and from the spot they are produced thus reducing the cost of processing, transportation and other taxes levied.

Advantages of Direct Marketing:

- The prospective buyers can be contacted directly making the recipient feel it is meant just for him/her.
- This saves costs of experimenting with n number of customers as it connects to the buyers who have been identified as likely to buy.
- For that reason it also has a higher return on investment, since the likelihood of making a sale to a targeted customer list is higher to begin with.
- It is measurable as it uses a number of built-in tools to track the success of each campaign, allowing the promoters to improve with each mail or email cycle. The impact of the direct marketing campaign has immediate results, and the costs and return from a direct marketing campaign can be measured.
- The campaigner has comprehensive control of the message and medium to be used to connect to the buyers.
- Customers and prospective customers are precisely targeted thus takes care of the traditional criticism of

direct mail, which is that many recipients do not want to receive unsolicited mails and messages.

Technology and its Applications in Marketing:

In the past 10 decades the innovations and advancements in technology have grown in multiples. The process of marketing has also undergone a complete change with the times from the barter exchanges to online and digitalized sale of goods and services. The hotels have introduced the 360 degree views in their websites to let the guests feel the actual ambience and all the facilities on offer in a short span of less than two minutes which cannot be expected to be done in the same duration by the staff in the hotel.

Digital Marketing is the new keyword for businesses as it has wider reach, takes lesser time and adds a quotient of genuineness to the offers with all FAQs available on site. This is a combination of many tools like content marketing, search engine optimization, internet and social media; popularly known as 360 degree marketing. Market research firms use and optimize these tools to gather data about likes and dislikes of all the individuals using the internet for searching the services or who are merely surfing the net for some information. This data is then automatically used to promote other relevant products and services to these users on the very next login.

Content Marketing:

The marketing activity focuses on specific content related to an issue or a specified area of interest. E.g. the hotel food blogs that have all the information related to the food served in the dining outlets with its history and other interesting facts about the cuisine. The website also has videos related to events and activities that are intended to create an interest for experiencing the same. These videos, articles and links are shared with prospective customers with an idea to keep them updated and also to motivate them to make purchases whenever any such need arises.

The advantages of content marketing are that it helps build credibility and trust with potential users by sharing complete information about a product's usage, features and how to get optimum output. Secondly the combination of content marketing and SEO leads to generation of more data and information which may be useful for a customer.

E.g. on a travel blog site if the difference between two adventure sport activities is discussed the reader might end up contacting the adventure resort and make a reservation.

Social Media:

Social media has replaced all other mediums in terms of sharing of information at lightning speed. The news, videos, articles, messages etc. get circulated within minutes to mass audience. The hospitality organization's and travel companies are also making use of social media to market their products and services. People from all genres are addicted to some or the other form of social media thus making it a useful platform for companies to promote their brands and services to all these users at no extra cost. Marketing is the reason that social media has been immensely popular for the creators of sites like Facebook and Instagram. The costs at times may be higher if the social media a popular one and also when a large audience is targeted but the return on investment is still higher than the traditional marketing methods.

Internet Branding:

The longer an advertisement stays on the social media or the internet the better it gets establishes the brand it represents. Every organization in business looks forward to get established as a brand and to be known as the one providing value for money. All the hotels irrespective of their size and locations are having their websites and offer online booking facilities to the guests. The competition is now on the quality of websites, the interactive prepositions, themes and layout for ease of navigation on the webpages. The websites have also to be mobile friendly as most of the people now connect to the internet through their cell phones.

Search Engine Optimization (SEO):

Digital marketing firms also have to account for SEO, as it is an important factor to determine how much exposure can be assured for their clients. SEO is a catch-all term that refers to all of the algorithms that go into determining what pops up on a search engine and in what order. Search Engine Optimization means controlling what content or brand gets reflected on the first page after a search in initiated by the user. The SEO providers have dedicated team members who work 24 X 7 to ensure that the brands they are working for are always on the first page. This is essential as in most cases the user does not wish to move beyond the first page. This mode creates and utilizes the appropriate keywords to promote the brands. SEO increases brands accessibility for an average person but it depends on the users who actively search for information.

Digital Signage:

The in-store or in-house promotions can use the digital signage as a crucial tool to market the day specials. This is particularly helpful for restaurants and other businesses that need to respond to changes in inventory or introduce new products on a regular basis. Advanced point of sale systems can give employees real-time information on what products are in stock or help them track a customer's preferences. Providing excellent customer service is a key to successful sales and marketing.

Cloud Computing:

This enables the marketing team members to communicate with each other in real time despite the physical distances between them. The quantum of data that can be stored and shared is much higher than the internet. This also brings in quality manpower from different parts of the world to work together on a common project which is difficult and expensive if they are made to work from a common office. Cloud computing has made it easier for the international hotel chain's properties to communicate with each other and to train the employees at different locations under the supervision of a trainer sitting in one of the hotels.

Big Data:

This is the assimilation of minutest details about the prospective consumers that helps companies identify the changes required in a product or service to make it popular and in turn generate higher revenue. By understanding the inclinations of these users a successful marketing plan can be drafted. More than 44% businesses are using big data to improve their sales and to prepare efficient marketing plans. The demand for a particular type of accommodation facility, cuisine, recreation and entertainment needs can be identified thru bug data analysis thus the hotel can prepare itself better than the competitors.

Internet of Things (IOT):

The IOT refers to the connectivity of the devices and appliances in user"s office and home. The internet of things assures facilities like switching on the lights and air conditioning units, temperature regulation, lighting adjustments to moods etc. from a distant location. Hotels are offering facilities to their guests by linking these facilities to the key cards and to the mobile phones of the resident guests.

SUMMARY:

In this chapter, we have discussed the meaning of Sales promotion, its objectives and how to select, develop and implement sales promotion strategies. More than any other element of the promotional mix, sales promotion is about "action". Sales promotion is the final marketing mix element. It is about stimulating customers to buy a product. It is not designed to be informative; a role which advertising is much better suited to. Sales promotion consists of short-term incentives to encourage purchase or sales of a product or service whereas advertising and personal selling offer reasons to buy a product or service, sales promotion offers reasons to buy now. Promotional strategy is the function of informing, persuading and influencing a consumer decision. It is as important to non-profit organizations as it is to a profit- oriented company like Colgate-Palmolive. Some promotional strategies are aimed at developing primary demand, the desire for a general product category.

Sales promotion activities may be used singly or in combination, both offensively and defensively, to achieve one goal or a set of goals. Sales-promotion tools vary in their specific objectives. A free sample stimulates consumer trial whereas a free management-advisory service aims at cementing a long-term relationship. Today, many marketing managers first estimate what they need to spend in trade promotion, then what they need to spend in consumer promotion. Whatever is left they will budget for advertising. There is a danger, however, in letting advertising take a back seat, because advertising typically acts to build brand loyalty. The question of whether or not sales promotion weakens brand loyalty is subject to opt for different interpretations. Sales promotion with its incessant price off, coupons, deals and premiums may devalue the product offering in buyers" mind. Buyers learn that the list price is largely a fiction. However, before jumping to any conclusion, we need to distinguish between price promotions and added-value promotions.

GLOSSARY:

- **Brand proliferation:** As companies are increasingly using branding to identify a product from competing products the number of brands has increased tremendously. Brands become less distinctive and product features cannot be advertised very effectively. Companies adopt sales promotion to ensure their share of the limited space with the retailers.
- **Change in attitudes:** Earlier, senior managements were of the view that sales promotion spoiled the image of their brand. But the success of competitors in sales promotion has made sales promotion more acceptable to such managements.
- **Competent staff:** Due to specialization, new staff positions have created in several companies. Executives with specialized qualifications have greater faith in modern techniques of sales promotion.

- **Coupons:** Certificates that offer buyers savings when they purchase specified products.
- **Dealer outlets:** A place where business for retailing goods is done.
- **Growth competition:** When one manufacturer adopts aggressive promotional strategy to create a brand image, the sales of other manufacturers are affected. In order to maintain their sales, other manufacturers also start sales promotion activities leading to virtually a promotion war.
- **Market share:** Ratio or area of a market controlled by a particular company or product.
- **Quick returns:** Sales promotion activities are launched quickly and yield faster. These activities also motivate the over burdened and lethargic sales force. Therefore, there is wide spread use of sales promotion schemes.
- **Recession:** During a recession, consumers can be persuaded to wait as during recession, business comes to zero. Therefore, manufacturers make use of these activities to reduce inventory and to improve cash position.
- **Sales promotion:** It consists of short-term incentives to encourage the purchase or sale of a product or service.
- **Seasonal products:** Those products whose demand varies in a regular pattern, season to season.
- **Trade pressure:** There is now greater pressure on manufacturers to provide support and allowances due to the growth of super market, chain assist retailers and thereby secure their cooperation.

The Author

Dr. Anshumali Pandey, is a renowned & reliable name in the field of Education, Hospitality, Tourism and Tribal Food. He is a Teacher and Chef by profession, and also an Author, a Business Auditor, and an avid culinary traveller to the Indian Sub continental hinterlands. Dr. Anshumali Pandey is a Hospitality Educator (PhD) who specialises in Higher Education, Office Administration, Pay roll, HR, Labour Laws, Audit, and Procurement & Tender Process. He is an Author with 47 Publications consisting of 32 Books.

The books written by Dr Anshumali Pandey are essentially a banquet arising from an experience of over 25 years of Professional life and have boiled down to crisp and accurate writing on his favourite subjects. Hospitality Sector champion requires to be a specialist in many fields and Dr Pandey is one of them. His knowledge is evident from the spectrum of subjects which he has chosen for his books so far, which ranges from being a specialist chef, to Master of Human resources, to Education and to love for children, and topped with Spirituality.

Books written by the Author are –

1. Theory of Indian Cookery
2. Beauty and Irony of Silvassa Tourism
3. A Short Indian Food Story
4. Be Your Own Guide to Indian Cuisine
5. Cookery Fundamentals
6. History of Indian Food
7. The Great Indian Story Book for Children
8. Personal Budget: Easy Work Book

9. Online Classes Log Book
10. Dictionary Making Work Book for School Children
11. The Lazy Bed
12. Hindu Dharm (हनि्दूधर्म) (In Hindi Language)
13. Where is my coffee?
14. Your First Job is Never your Last (Volume 1)
15. You are Almost There (Quick Fix Resume and Interview Hacks)
16. Working for the Enemy? - A lesson in Career Management
17. Public Speaking for the Young
18. A Date With Coffee
19. How to be The Best Hotel Front Office Employee
20. Diploma in Food Production, The complete Syllabus
21. Diploma in F&B Service, The Complete Syllabus
22. Diploma in Front Office, The Complete Syllabus
23. The Time to Speak is Now
24. Munshi Premchand (Short Stories in English)
25. The Housekeeping Department, Text Book
26. Hitchhiker's Guide to Trekking in Uttarakhand
27. Uttarakhand, A divine Land for a Reason
28. Bachhon ke liye rochak kahaniyan (बच्चों के लिए रोचक कहानियाँ) (In Hindi Language)
29. Basic Communication Skills of English
30. The Basic Office Organisation Book for Start-ups
31. Hospitality HRM
32. Hospitality Marketing

Connect with me: anshumali.pandey@gmail.com
https://notionpress.com/author/337004

Dr Anshumali Pandey, PhD, Author.

Scan the QR code to check latest updates of the Author's works.

www.ingramcontent.com/pod-product-compliance
Ingram Content Group UK Ltd.
Pitfield, Milton Keynes, MK11 3LW, UK
UKHW041955190726
13854UKWH00005B/1992